THE TEMPLETON PLAN

THE

TEMPLETON

PLAN

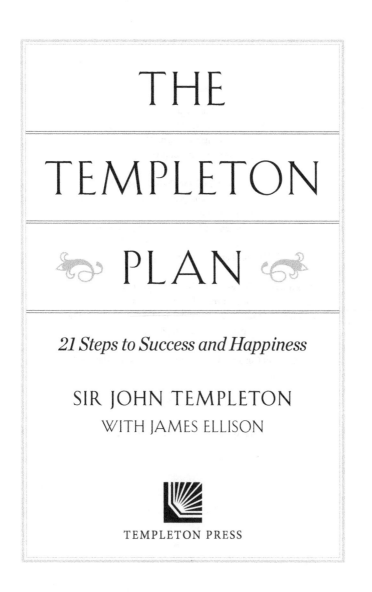

21 Steps to Success and Happiness

SIR JOHN TEMPLETON
WITH JAMES ELLISON

TEMPLETON PRESS

Templeton Press
300 Conshohocken State Road, Suite 500
West Conshohocken, PA 19428
www.templetonpress.org

2013 Templeton Press Edition
A Giniger Book

Designed and typeset by Gopa & Ted2, Inc.

Library of Congress Cataloging-in-Publication Data on file.

Printed in the United States of America

13 14 15 16 17 18 10 9 8 7 6 5 4 3 2

For Irene, whose deep spirituality and natural beauty of character are ever a source of joy to me.

Sir John Templeton

CONTENTS

Foreword by Sir John Templeton ix

Introduction by James Ellison xi

STEP 1 Learning the Laws of Life 3

STEP 2 Using What You Have 11

STEP 3 Helping Yourself by Helping Others 20

STEP 4 Putting First Things First 25

STEP 5 Achieving Happiness by What You Do 29

STEP 6 Finding the Positive in Every Negative 41

STEP 7 Investing Yourself in Your Work 53

STEP 8 Creating Your Own Luck 67

STEP 9 Utilizing Two Principles of Success 75

STEP 10 Making Time Your Servant 83

STEP 11 Giving the Extra Ounce 88

STEP 12 Conserving Your Resources to Best Advantage 96

STEP 13 Progressing Onwards and Upwards 109

STEP 14 Controlling Your Thoughts for Effective Action 118

STEP 15 Loving as the Essential Ingredient 127

STEP 16 Maximizing the Power of Your Faith 133

STEP 17 Receiving Strength through Prayer 139

STEP 18 Giving as a Way of Life 145

STEP 19 Winning through Humility 155

STEP 20 Discovering New Frontiers 161

STEP 21 Seeking Solutions 170

Summing Up the Templeton Plan 179

FOREWORD

The Templeton Plan came into being out of my concern that no book had created a set of rules to help readers increase their quotient of happiness and prosperity. I know that my life would have been more useful and fulfilled had I learned at an earlier age the principles described here. The twenty-one steps of The Templeton Plan could have provided me and others of my generation with clearer guideposts to success.

James Ellison relates lucidly the ideas and experiences I shared with him in the course of many interviews. During my seventy-four years I have made my share of mistakes, but Mr. Ellison thought it best to stress those experiences and thoughts from which the reader may derive a useful lesson. To overcome the problems that each one of us faces—and no life is problem-free—it is crucial to have a plan to live by.

The plan this book suggests is by no means complete. Many principles for a happy and successful existence—what you might call the "laws of life"—are not included because I have not yet learned them. *The Templeton Plan* is written for those who consider themselves students in the school of total success. Each student should study the twenty-one steps included here and then try to add to them. Nothing can be more beneficial for your spiritual growth than to put down in writing what you believe are the most important laws for happiness, usefulness, and success.

I am convinced that the basic principles for happiness and success can be examined, tested, and agreed upon so that the best ones can be combined into textbooks for teaching in schools. No subject in the curriculum would seem more important than one that can help us fulfill our potential as human beings.

It is my vision that more and more people worldwide will lead lives of happiness, usefulness, and prosperity if we work continuously toward spiritual growth and better understanding of the virtues by which we should govern ourselves. And it is my hope that not only each of us but also our children and grandchildren will one day benefit from reading this book.

Sir John Templeton

INTRODUCTION

John Marks Templeton, regarded by Wall Street as one of the world's wisest investors, is the founder of the Templeton mutual fund group, which now manages more than $6 billion owned by more than 500,000 public investors. He started his investment career on a borrowed $10,000 and thus is a living embarrassment to the efficient market theory, which holds that you cannot start from nothing and end up with a large fortune in a single lifetime.

Forbes magazine has dubbed him "one of the handful of true investment greats in a field crowded with mediocrity and bloated reputations." Templeton believes that successful investing is a product of a person's overall relationship to life and to the universe. Unlike most people, he is at peace with himself. He has sorted the important questions out. He believes that God created and is continuously creating the universe.

While many people hold that financial success is separate from religious belief, that in fact there is a conflict between the two, it is John Templeton's conviction that the two are related. He contends that the most successful people are often the most religiously motivated. They are likely to have the keenest understanding of the importance of ethics in business. They can be trusted to give full measure and not cheat their customers.

In trying to appraise the value of a corporation, which is the heart of selecting investment bargains, nothing is more important than the quality of the management. Each year, Templeton and his associates study hundreds of corporations to determine which ones offer the best opportunities for their clients. They have found that the common denominator connecting successful people and successful enterprises is a devotion to ethical and spiritual principles.

When John Templeton first became a trustee at the Princeton Theological Seminary thirty-six years ago, there was another trustee named John J. Newberry. As a young man, Newberry had worked for F. W. Woolworth. When he left to open his first J. J. Newberry store, he instituted the practice of daily prayer meetings. Newberry hired people who wanted to open each working day with prayer. Throughout the day, they usually did a better job for customers because they began with a better attitude. The Newberry chain spread rapidly until it included hundreds of stores.

For John Templeton there is no special magic in this remarkable success story. He is convinced that you can credit a significant part of Newberry's success to the prayer meetings with which he opened each store each morning.

J. C. Penney, a devout Christian, built up one of the largest retail organizations in the world, based squarely on the principles of brotherhood and a belief in God. Sam Walton, the originator of Wal-Mart stores in Arkansas and a fabulous Wall Street success story, was another who founded his business on Christian attitudes with both customers and employees. No other retail organization over the past thirty years could rival Wal-Mart's steady and consistent growth.

At Templeton, all of the directors' and shareholders' meetings open with prayer. But prayer is never used as an aid in making specific stock selections. "That would be a gross misinterpretation of God's methods," Templeton says. "What we do pray for is wisdom. We pray that the decisions we make today will be wise decisions and that our talks about different stocks will be wise talks. Of course, our discussions and decisions are fallible and sometimes flawed. No one should expect that, just because he begins with prayer, every decision he makes is going to be profitable. However, I do believe that, if you pray, you will make fewer stupid mistakes."

Tales of the Templeton wizardry are often told in dollar-growth figures. For example, where would you be today if you had put $10,000 into his first mutual fund in 1954? Your investment, including reinvestment distributions, would have grown to more than $800,000 by 1987! That's how successful the Templeton technique has been over a thirty-two-year period.

And to what does Templeton credit this remarkable growth? "Backed by our beliefs," he says, "we're not so uptight and on edge as those who are in the business merely to make money. We start each day by setting our minds on the important things and praying. All our transactions are influenced by that.

"There are businesses that apply the *un*-Christian principle. They ignore the human factor. They lack the wholehearted desire to offer better service and higher quality at lower prices. More often than not, those businesses fail. In general, people who take advantage in their dealings will get a bad reputation and before long others will not want to deal with them.

"That greed and callousness are shortsighted business methods is a crucial lesson for us all to absorb. Learning it will spell success. You should always care about your customer. You should treat your employee as you want to be treated. If you follow those precepts, which are rooted in religion, financial success is likely to follow."

The purpose of The Templeton Plan is to reveal the vital connections between belief in religious principles and belief in oneself that will enable you to become a successful and happy person. Through Templeton's twenty-one-step program that follows, you will learn how the person who lives by God's principles is the same person who will succeed in life, making lasting friendships and most likely reaping significant financial rewards.

It is suggested that you devote yourself to one step each day, over a period of three weeks. Each step should be studied carefully until the following questions can be answered in a satisfactory and thorough manner:

1. What do these ideas really mean?
2. How do they apply to my own life?
3. How can I use their meaning in achieving success?

The Templeton Plan: 21 Steps to Success and Happiness has worked for many people—for John Templeton himself and for others. There is no reason that it cannot work for you.

James Ellison, 1987

THE TEMPLETON PLAN

STEP 1

LEARNING THE LAWS OF LIFE

THE WORLD OPERATES on spiritual principles, just as it does on the laws of physics and gravity. These principles, or laws, are as important for our welfare as stopping for a red light at a busy intersection. Our inner life is saved or lost to the extent that we obey or disobey the laws of life.

These laws are the underpinning of The Templeton Plan. We will examine them now, at the start, so that we can have a clear idea of our direction. Just as a baby learns to walk by taking one step at a time, so we will look at the laws of life one at a time to assess the ground that will be covered in our twenty-one steps.

Truthfulness is a law of life. In the farming community where John Templeton grew up, there was a general saying that your word was your bond. People of character would never promise something and then go back on their word. A contract between two parties did not have to be put into writing; there was no need for a court or a judge to enforce it. Civilization, as it was then perceived by many, was a place where the handshake was sacred.

Reliability is a law of life. The shopkeeper or professional who prospers today is the one whose word you can depend on. If he says he will have a certain product available for you Tuesday afternoon, he will have it Tuesday afternoon. If she tells you the product is genuine leather, you can rest assured that genuine leather is what you'll get.

Faithfulness is a law of life. You expect people not to cheat you or put themselves ahead of you. Faithfulness means that they will be faithful to their trust. You can rely on them not to cut corners or try to deceive you.

Perseverance is a law of life. You will always give your business and your trust to those who will see a project through even if difficulties arise—and they usually do. In everything we do, there are problems to solve, and the person who gives up or turns to an easier task is not the kind of person who will find success.

Thirty-six years ago, John Templeton helped to found the Young Presidents' Organization, a worldwide club. Each of the thousands of members, though they come from a wide range of cultural and economic backgrounds, before age forty became president of a company employing over a hundred people. What do these men and women have in common? "Perseverance," Templeton explains. "When they undertake to accomplish something, they accomplish it. The program may change along the way, but they don't give up."

Enthusiasm is a law of life. To be a success you must work at a task with your whole heart. Enthusiasm is contagious. You can infect your suppliers and customers with it.

Energy is a law of life. Successful, deeply fulfilled people have a high degree of energy. They are not lazy, nor do they spend much time on idle matters. They are constantly trying new things, experimenting, searching for a cheaper method of production or for ways to improve the quality of a product.

Humility is a law of life. The young should welcome, not ignore, the advice and experience of their teachers and parents. The majority of parents discipline their children because they love them and want the best for them. For children to rebel against their teachers and parents flies in the face of the simplest common sense. The teacher is in school to help students; students should be humble enough to realize that the teacher knows more than they do. Through a humble approach to life, the successful person will learn at an early age to profit from the knowledge of parents and teachers.

Pleasing others is a law of life. Now, of course, it's impossible to please everyone, but we will be more productive and successful if we try. That means pleasing your colleagues, pleasing your clients and customers. The concept of giving pleasure to others is having a healthy new influence on the business world. There are now dozens of service clubs where businesspeople gather as equals once a week to discuss mutual concerns—the Rotary and Kiwanis clubs, among others. As an old Oriental proverb has it, "If you wish your merit to be known, acknowledge that of other people."

Giving is a law of life. Successful people give and give

still more; their giving is returned to them in full measure. Watch the top people in business. They are the ones who give more than is expected of them. In return, they receive the rewards. They attract the customers. Their giving leads ultimately to success, both in worldly and spiritual terms.

John Templeton serves on the board of corporators of the oldest corporation in the United States, the Presbyterian Ministers' Fund. It is a life insurance company that insures the lives of ministers of all faiths. The company seal carries a drawing of the sower. The Presbyterian Fund has enjoyed considerable success for more than two centuries. They have given their policyholders more insurance for a lower price than other companies. And their representatives, who are usually Christian ministers, never fail to explain to prospective clients that the fund is founded on the concept that as you sow, so shall you reap.

Learning from others is a law of life. As a child, John Templeton used to observe his schoolmates as well as the adults with whom he came in contact. He watched the farmers in the country. He learned from each of them which things led to success, happiness, and productivity and which did not. He learned what to emulate as well as what to avoid. Most important, he learned to assimilate the wisdom of many lives. You can do the same. If you're alert, it is possible to learn from each person you meet, to avoid mistakes, and to put new virtues into practice.

Joy is a law of life. John Templeton names as the most joyful group of people he has ever met the young women studying to be members of the society of Mother Teresa. He observed that their happiness had an almost visible glow, and it had nothing to do with self-indulgence. They were happy because of the opportunity to serve.

While Templeton was attending the twenty-fifth anniversary of Mother Teresa's order, the Missionaries of Charity, in Calcutta, a young novice approached Mother Teresa and in an overjoyed manner cried out, "Mother, for six hours I've been handling the body of Christ!" She meant that she had found a man in the street whose condition was so bad that it took her six hours to get him cleaned up, comfortable, and in bed. She felt that Christ had come to her in the form of that man. What a joy it was that she could be useful, that she was in a position to help Christ when he came to her in need. Success need not necessarily take a financial form. But real success can never be achieved without the element of usefulness, of serving.

Altruism is a law of life. The altruistic person tries to make our world a better place to live in. There are medical researchers who have improved our lot by discovering penicillin or insulin. Every person—each in his or her own way—can make the world a better place. Those who search for success and happiness will find a way. One man makes the world a better place by developing his farm with more modern agricultural methods. Another man, a widower, raises his six children on his own. They love him so much that, when they marry, they live near home so that the family needn't split apart. That man made the world a better place by loving his six children. They had the benefit and warmth of his love, and that is a form of riches that is always passed on.

The altruist discovers an individual way to make the world a better place than it was before. It may be because he writes a book. Or because she paints a picture. Or because he rears his children with intelligence and compassion. Or because she invents a new cooking recipe. Or because his life serves as a shining light for others. There are large and small ways to make the world a better place, and all the paths, as different as they may be, lead to success.

Templeton recalls a school near where he grew up in Winchester, Tennessee, that tried to teach more than reading, writing, and arithmetic. The Webb School was started by an elderly man named Shaunee Webb. The motto of the school was "We Teach Character." Webb regarded it as his principal purpose to teach students the laws of life along with Latin, history, and mathematics. Many graduates of the Webb School became nationally known, their success based on what they learned from the founder.

Templeton says: "I am now offering prizes for the best essays on the laws of life, written by high school and college students. My hope is that this will create a beautiful snowball effect. The students writing the essays will have to read extensively in the fields of ethics, religion, and philosophy. Consequently, at a very young age, they will have formulated their own laws and will learn to focus on them. When the prizewinning essays are published, they will reach others, and gradually a literature on the laws of life can be built up.

"Taking that thought a step further, it might even be possible to develop a world council on the laws of life. I believe there are such laws that every religion believes in. We might thereby produce a world view, thus eliminating conflicts between individuals and even nations, because we will have developed a more sophisticated understanding of the principles that unify us.

"My guess is that there are literally hundreds of such laws that can be agreed on by 99 percent of all people. It would then be possible to prepare textbooks for high schools and colleges so that there could be courses on the laws of life. I believe that such a program would help religions and governments to cooperate with one another more easily."

Step 1 teaches you to study the laws of life as you proceed on the road to success and happiness. Study those you know and search for new ones. The list of those laws we have examined is small:

Truthfulness
Reliability
Faithfulness
Perseverance
Enthusiasm
Energy
Humility
Pleasing others
Giving
Learning from others
Joy
Altruism

There are many more laws, perhaps hundreds more. Start with these twelve and apply the meaning of each law to your own life. Are you lacking in energy? Could you use an extra dose of enthusiasm? Consider this a checklist to use to monitor your own strengths and weaknesses. Remember: The laws of life are the basic building blocks for a successful and happy life.

STEP 2

USING WHAT YOU HAVE

DURING JOHN TEMPLETON'S four decades as an investment counselor, he has seen many families who have left their children great wealth. But that kind of inheritance can create more problems than it solves. He likes to quote the founder of Pennsylvania, William Penn, who said, "He who is taught to live upon little owes more to his father's wisdom than he who has a great deal left him does to his father's care."

In studying hundreds of clients, Templeton has never been able to discern a connection between happiness and inherited wealth. In fact, in most cases the inheritance of wealth has done more harm than good. It tends to give people false values and causes them to show personal pride without having earned that pride. It causes people to take the edge off their efforts.

Templeton is convinced that the young should earn their own spending money. A child needs to learn to work as early as six years old. Although it takes an expenditure of time and imagination for the parent to figure out what a child of six can do that is useful, there are many activities that will teach a child the meaning of pride in work. In the country, children can tend a lemonade stand, or grow radishes to sell to the grocery store, or collect cans for the return of the deposit. In the city, children can be assigned chores around the apartment.

Templeton, who grew up in the rural South, feels that it's rare for a country child to get in trouble with the law later in life. On a farm, children can feed the farm animals or help with the preparation of food; they are more likely than their city counterparts to become useful members of the family at a very young age. As a result, they will mature earlier and have a firmer grasp of the laws of life.

Contrary to current psychological opinion, children in many respects are miniature adults. They have a burning desire to stand on their own two feet. Thus, when a mother does her daughter's homework, feeling she's helping the child, she is actually doing her harm in the long run. Granted, the child will get good grades the next day in school. But it's far better to take the longer and more arduous route and show the girl how to do the long division herself. She will then have more personal pride and self-confidence, feel more adult, and be better able to take the next step in school, because today's lesson is based on what was learned the previous day. If the mother causes her daughter to miss out on that single step in her progress, then the daughter may have trouble picking it up later.

As mentioned in Step 1, the successful person learns from others. By careful observation, you can monitor the mistakes of others and not make them yourself. You can also begin to see who is happy and why they are happy. Train yourself to watch those in your school, at your place of employment, in your own family. And listen to what they say. Listening intelligently is a key to success, because you are storing up the wisdom and the folly of others and beginning to discriminate between the two.

Never forget that learning is a lifetime activity of vast importance. John Templeton recalls a friend from his high school who, upon graduating, got a job and never read another book. He watched television in his spare time, went to movies, did some hunting and fishing, but made no effort to expand the frontiers of his mind. At age forty, he was no better educated than he'd been at sixteen, and that's the sign of a wasted life. Wasted lives are never successful lives.

In fact, we're in a position to learn more once we're out of school, because school is a kind of hothouse environment; it is later, out in the world, that we meet the realities of life. Once we are involved in the world of work, books should take on an even greater importance. We can test them against our greater maturity and knowledge. We can absorb their messages with a more profound understanding.

Years ago John Templeton set himself a goal to learn something new each day. It is important not to let a day go by without learning the meaning of an unfamiliar word, without a new insight, without experiencing a fresh taste, thought, or sensation. If you travel to your job by bus, watch the other passengers. You will discover that the majority of them do absolutely nothing. They simply sit there. Are they thinking something significant? Are they working out a problem? The chances are they are letting time die, unused.

But those who are going to get ahead, who will achieve success, will refuse to waste their moments on that bus. They will study. They will read or write. They will use their time, to and from school or work, for self-improvement, production, and continued learning.

By listening to the passengers on that bus you can guess with fair accuracy who is going to achieve success and who is not. If you hear someone saying that "he said so and so and she said so and so and then he said so and so," you can bet that person is not forging ahead. But the one who is saying that "this is what I learned yesterday; this is what I hope to accomplish today" is a person on the road to success.

Besides perfecting the art of listening, the successful person is the one who asks questions. You don't learn much if you're doing the talking. Form the habit of asking yourself, "What can I learn from this person?" Discover what the individual likes to talk about and then ask questions in that area of interest. This practice will pay off in two ways: You will please the person by asking intelligent questions and at the same time you will learn something yourself.

Successful people seek advice more often than they give it. John Templeton gives an illustration of this strategy from his days as a young man working for the National Geophysical Company in Dallas, Texas. It was his first major job after college and he was bent on succeeding. At least once a month he approached his employer and said, "What can I do to improve my work?" Again, there was a twofold benefit: While Templeton learned how to do a better job, his boss realized how sincere he was in his desire to improve. Within a year, he became financial vice-president of the company; the key to his advancement, he's convinced, was his attitude of constantly asking questions.

The question "What would you do if you were me?" is a stepping-stone toward success. By asking that question, you'll not only get creative suggestions but other people will realize that you're the type of person whose career course is decidedly on the upward swing.

A candidate for success should always carry a library. You can make the minutes count, whether waiting at the airport to board an airplane or holding on to a strap on the subway. You may be catching up on office work, or analyzing current events, or simply reading to improve your mind and widen your knowledge.

If you arrive early for an appointment, you can have papers to occupy you while you wait. By having books and papers with you at all times—your portable library—you can always accomplish something that will advance your career that much more quickly.

Success comes more easily to those who were given sound role models. John Templeton was most fortunate in that respect. He was born into a family of modest means in the small town of Winchester, Tennessee. His father, Harvey Maxwell Templeton, was a lawyer by profession, even though he'd never attended college. But, in a town of fewer than 2,000 people, you couldn't earn a living from legal work alone. Showing the entrepreneurial flair that would become his son's trademark, he built and operated a cotton gin, which sometimes produced as many as 2,000 bales of cotton in one season. Even though the farmers paid Harvey only two dollars a bale, that was enough to support the Templeton family throughout the year.

But it was only a beginning. Like his son, Harvey Templeton was never satisfied with less than the utmost effort.

His business led to a cotton storage venture, to fertilizer retailing, to profitable speculation on the New York and New Orleans cotton exchanges. Young John listened eagerly to tales of the wheeling and dealing that engaged much of his father's attention each week.

Nor did Harvey Templeton stop there.

He was also an agent for a number of insurance companies. He was acutely sensitive to ways he could profit from the rise and fall of the rural economy in his section of Tennessee. When farms came up for auction because of nonpayment of real estate taxes, he would buy a farm if the price was unusually low. He would then plan to resell the farm for a profit at a later date.

Young John was always watching and evaluating his father's enterprises. John's convictions about the hazards of incurring debt were reinforced as he saw many farmers losing their land at auction. And his natural inclination toward independence and self-reliance grew stronger as he saw the excitement and potential profit that accompanied his father's business activities.

By 1925 Harvey Templeton owned six farms, in addition to his cotton gin, legal work, and other business activities. Also, by using low-cost surplus lumber and workmen who couldn't find other jobs, he was able to build about two dozen small homes on his growing real estate holdings. He then rented them for from two to six dollars a month—a good return on houses that cost only $200–$500 to build.

John Templeton learned the uses of ambition and drive from his father, who provided a relatively good living for his family during hard times. Even though they were not wealthy by the outside world's standards, they were the second family in the county to own both a telephone and an automobile. And, significant for John's development, year by year he observed a gradual increase in the family's financial position through his father's hard work and creative business flair.

But his father was only half of John Templeton's background.

John's mother, Vella, provided a quite different—but equally important—example for John to incorporate into his own personality. First of all, she was very well educated among women of that era. She had attended grammar school and high school in Winchester, and then she went on to study mathematics, Greek, and Latin for more than seven years at the Winchester Normal College.

Vella's interests were as wide-ranging as her husband's.

Though well educated and an intellectual by inclination, she enjoyed raising chickens, cows, and pigs. She enjoyed gardening and raised peaches, corn, cabbage, cherries, asparagus, and green beans. The Templeton table was always well supplied with fresh vegetables, meat, and dairy products.

Young John, along with his brother Harvey Jr., was often underfoot as his mother went about her daily tasks. And it was in this environment that he learned his first important lesson about profits—at the age of four.

To start with, he found that, with a little work, he could grow his own beans in his mother's garden at a cost of next to nothing for the seeds. Then he could sell the beans to a local country store for a handsome profit.

John came up with the idea of selling produce on his own. His mother allowed him the freedom to set up his little business, but the outside advice and direction ended there. From then on, he was on his own.

The practical business savvy that young Templeton inherited from his father was clearly one aspect of his inheritance. But his mother's influence was crucial in bringing precocious financial achievement into perfect balance with sound spiritual values. John learned early from his mother that the content of his character could lead either to success or failure. His mother and his aunt Leila taught him how right thoughts can forge right actions. For a number of years they kept the Cumberland Presbyterian church going by raising enough money to pay the part-time minister. Thus they taught this future investment genius a valuable lesson on different ways to raise money and what money, once earned, can do to help others. It is clear that, in John Templeton's case, his background helped point the way to success.

But success is never a legacy. It must be earned by each individual on his or her own terms. Although young John was given a better start than many, like all of us he had a long way to go before, through growth and transformation, he could truly call himself a successful human being.

A careful reading of Step 2 should help you to raise your success and happiness quotient. Try to follow these rules:

1. Discover your strengths and then use them to the best advantage.
2. Listen to others and learn from them.
3. Observe the actions of others so that you can profit from both their strengths and their mistakes.
4. Do not wait for goals to materialize but go out and actively seek goals.
5. Money can be inherited but never success. It must be earned by each individual.
6. The surest way to achieve success is to emulate sound role models, whether they be your parents, your teachers, your friends, or your business associates.

STEP 3

HELPING YOURSELF BY HELPING OTHERS

When people hear the word *ministry*, they automatically think of a church or government office. But, in truth, everything productive that you can accomplish in life is a ministry. If you make shoes that last, you have performed a ministry. It's a ministry to produce a bountiful harvest. If you're an internist who saves lives or a novelist who creates beauty, then that too is a ministry.

Because your ministry is also your livelihood, choose with care. Make certain that you love what you do. By loving your work, by taking the attitude that it should be done on behalf of others, you'll be doing it as a ministry. You will be creating something that the world needs—which is dedication to the job at hand—and that makes you a genuine minister. As a giver, a helper, you are much more likely to be successful than the person who works simply to earn a living. You will make more money and receive greater recognition.

The more one works and plants, the more one will harvest. The more good one can do, the more success one can achieve. Perhaps this is best explained by Jesus in the Bible parable of the talents. To quote John Templeton, who likes to tell his own version of the story: "A man going on a trip entrusted his property to his servants. He gave one man five talents, another two, and another one, each according to his abilities. While he was gone, the man with five talents traded with his money and made five talents more. And the man with two talents traded his and made an additional two talents. But the man with one talent buried his master's money in the ground.

"When the master returned, he went over his accounts with his three servants. The man entrusted with five talents explained that he'd invested and made five more. And the man given two talents also showed how he'd put his talents to work and now had four talents. The master complimented them both, told them that they had been faithful servants, and that he would entrust them with greater responsibilities.

"The man with one talent came forward and said, 'Master, I figured you're a hard man and you might rob me of my earnings, so I hid this money in the ground.'

"His master replied, 'You're a wicked and lazy slave. You knew I'd demand your profit. You should have put my money in the bank where it would draw interest. Give your money to the man with ten talents. For to the man who has will be given more. And from the man who has nothing, even his nothing will be taken away!'"

In New Testament times, a silver talent was valuable currency, worth well over a thousand of today's dollars. But Jesus spoke in parables and he used them to veil the truth from those who were not willing to see it. Those, on the other hand, who were zealous for the truth would not rest until they had found out his meaning. Thus the talent certainly stood for something else, something with a more spiritual weight than money alone. Many people, Templeton among them, believe that the talents Jesus spoke of were literally abilities that God bestowed on each individual human being—few in some cases, many in others.

For John Templeton, nothing in his religious training had more influence on him than the parable of the talents. What exactly did he learn from it? He learned that God gives talents to each of us. He also learned that God hands these talents out in uneven measure. But, although God may have given more talents to one person than another, he expects everyone to use those they have to the utmost, no matter how great or meager they might be, and to use them in the service of others. The point is simply this: God is responsible for what talents you possess. From there on, the responsibility is yours. You have to develop them as far and as deeply as they will go. And the people who use their talents completely—and most of all to help others less fortunate—will be rewarded. Those people will find success.

At least ninety-nine people out of a hundred are born into the world with talents that can be developed. Most of us are given more talents than we realize, and it's up to us to mine those at which we'll be best. Also, in developing your own talents, you should help other people develop theirs. The great ministry is not to build yourself into a model but to help others discover and develop their abilities, to help yourself by helping them. Sometimes people don't know their own worth and need praise and encouragement.

An illustration of this is the story about a priest named Bourne, counseling an unhappy man who claimed to have no talents. The priest disputed him. He said, "As long as you are able to speak to me, you are not one of those people. Anyone who can carry on a conversation has been given a talent. Suppose your talent is to keep a street clean. Suppose that's your chief qualification in life. So go ahead and clean that street. Clean it with love and care to make others happy as they walk on it. Then, as your talent for cleaning that street grows, it should become a famous street."

When he first heard this story, Templeton thought of the street as Bourne Street, after the priest who encouraged the man. He says that if he were given that one talent, he would have tourists coming from hundreds of miles around to marvel at his clean street, and in its glory it would be renamed Bourne.

Success takes many forms; wealth and fame are only one kind of success. Perhaps you have a talent to help those who have no talents. There are such people. For example, the severely brain-damaged are unable to develop talents; taking care of them can help us to grow by helping them to function.

The aged and infirm, the mentally and physically handicapped, those beyond hope and caught in the coils of mental disease—they are the people who teach us the meaning of spiritual principles. John Templeton knows a Christian minister who was awarded grants from the federal government to maintain a home for sixteen severely mentally retarded people. Through his efforts, all sixteen have developed at least minimal abilities: Some wait on tables and carry out garbage, others plant vegetables and mow lawns. That Christian minister may not have large bank accounts and a Rolls-Royce. Nonetheless, he is among the richest and most successful of men.

Every act of helping is a way of saying yes to life. And saying yes is a profound form of successful behavior and happiness.

Step 3 suggests the following course of action:

1. Explore your talents carefully; choose your career with care; make certain you love what you do.
2. Share your talents in ways that truly benefit others, particularly the less fortunate.
3. Develop an attitude of greatness by applying the "Bourne" principle.
4. Share your greatness, as described in the "Bourne" example, with others.

Ask yourself these two key questions:

- Am I doing the thing that I am best qualified to do?
- Is my work helping me by helping at least one other human being?

STEP 4

PUTTING FIRST THINGS FIRST

All of us believe in virtue, but few of us give much thought to the varieties of virtue that exist and to their relative spiritual weights. One of the best methods for examining virtues is to try to decide in your own mind which virtues you think are the most important. Draw up a list of them. What virtue would you put first? In what order would you assign their importance? No two people will compile the same list, but the effort of preparing it will help you clarify your thinking.

All of us have been taught that crime does not pay and, of course, it's true. Crime of any kind is a sin and leads to failure. The virtues provide the underpinning for success in life, both in business and spiritually. Study the virtues. Start family discussions around the dining room table, having each member draw up his or her list of virtues. This can also be done in college classrooms, or at church prayer meetings, or wherever people gather socially. Encourage others to draw up their own list of virtues in order of importance. There is no surer way of growing spiritually than to discuss and study priorities in the field of virtues.

The purpose of The Templeton Plan is to help people

become successful in the full sense of that word. No matter what career you might embark on, success comes from knowing the importance of the virtues. It is not enough to live them unconsciously; you must struggle to know them and live them consciously.

Each person will have a different list of virtues, with different priorities. It will be helpful to discuss virtues with people who have viewpoints different from yours. By exchanging viewpoints on virtues, everyone can grow more open-minded and productive.

Here is the start of a list, which you can add to and change as you produce your own:

- gentleness,
- humility,
- self-control,
- hopefulness,
- perseverance,
- enthusiasm,
- responsibility,
- farsightedness,
- unselfishness,
- honor,
- hard work,
- generosity,
- promptness,
- thrift,
- originality,
- judgment,
- calmness,
- loyalty,
- forgiveness,
- thanksgiving,
- common sense,
- honesty,
- bravery,
- and love.

This is by no means a complete list. But it's a beginning. We all learn by setting down our own priorities in virtues. John Templeton discussed the priority of virtues with an acquaintance who placed labor at the top of her list. That told him a lot about the woman. It also made him consider labor in the vast scheme of virtues.

Another friend of Templeton's ranked loyalty first on his

list. Templeton asked him for an example of what he meant by loyalty. His friend explained that he could think of nothing more beautiful than a married couple celebrating their golden wedding anniversary—two people having lived fifty years of their life together. This example was at the root of his concept of loyalty.

Still another friend of Templeton's, Royal Little, a successful businessman now in his nineties, assigns great importance to the virtue of modesty. He believes that a man must be willing to admit his mistakes and deflate his own balloon before he can call himself truly successful. Little actually wrote a book called *How to Lose a Hundred Million Dollars and Other Valuable Advice.*

Here is a member of the Business Hall of Fame, a man who built a great corporation called Textron and later a company called Narragansett Capital, a man who is widely regarded as the originator of the conglomerate—a man famous in his field. And yet what is the subject of his book? He writes of his mistakes and of what he tried to learn from his mistakes. When discussing the book with Templeton, he said that many of his friends had written books detailing all the things they had done right, but he thought it would be much more helpful to the public to read about his various disasters. So he assembled forty different mistakes he had made in his career and explained to the reader what he had learned from each mistake.

Thus the importance of modesty as a virtue. Through the example of this multimillionaire businessman we have a much clearer sense of what modesty can actually mean in practice and how, like all of the virtues, it can promote success. John Templeton himself, in fact, wrote a book entitled *The Humble Approach.*

Templeton has been a sharp observer of people all his life. During the thirty-seven years since he helped form the Young Presidents' Organization, whose members were leaders in their fields, he watched these people carefully and studied their virtues. He believes that the virtues most visible among them were responsibility, energy, hard work, enthusiasm, and perseverance. Although he does not necessarily assign them the highest rank among the virtues, he is convinced they are significantly present in almost every prime candidate for success.

To successfully complete Step 4, try to answer the following questions:

1. List all the virtues that have special meaning for you.
2. Rank them in order of importance in your life.
3. Think of examples where you have been able to put various virtues into practice.
4. Discuss virtues with family members, business associates, and friends. They may provide you with insights into the virtues you need to practice to lead a happy and successful life.

STEP 5

ACHIEVING HAPPINESS BY WHAT YOU DO

John Templeton is fond of quoting financier Charles H. Burr, who said: "Getters don't get happiness; givers get it. You simply give to others a bit of yourself—a thoughtful act, a helpful idea, a word of appreciation, a lift over a rough spot, a sense of understanding, a timely suggestion. You take something out of your mind, garnished in kindness out of your heart, and put it into the other fellow's mind and heart."

And the world-famous philosopher and physician Dr. Albert Schweitzer: "I don't know what your destiny will be, but one thing I know: The only ones among you who will be really happy are those who will have sought and found how to serve."

And Henry Ward Beecher, the religious leader and social reformer: "No man can tell whether he is rich or poor by turning to his ledger. It is the heart that makes a man rich. He is rich according to what he is, not according to what he has."

And the author Sidney Powell: "Try to forget yourself in

the service of others. For when we think too much of ourselves and our own interests, we easily become dependent."

Hugh Black, who was for thirty years professor of practical theology at the Union Theological Seminary in New York: "It is the paradox of life that the way to miss pleasure is to seek it first. The very first condition of lasting happiness is that a life should be full of purpose, aiming at something outside self. As a matter of experience, we find that true happiness comes in seeking other things, in the manifold activities of life, in the healthful outgoing of all human powers."

And Robert J. McCracken, then pastor of New York City's Riverside Church: "The most infectiously joyous men and women are those who forget themselves in thinking about others and serving others. Happiness comes not by deliberately courting and wooing it but by giving oneself in self-effacing surrender to great values."

The American Declaration of Independence states that the pursuit of happiness is an inalienable right, but the pursuit of happiness is never successful. The more you pursue it, the less it will be achieved, and the less your success will be assured.

The way to capture happiness is to try to do something not directly aimed at giving you pleasure. Then happiness will come to you. If you develop your talents and become excellent at a particular line of work, you will realize happiness and success. Happiness and success are awarded to those who do not seek them as ends in themselves but struggle to excel at a given task. If you try to help someone else achieve happiness, happiness will come to you.

We have all heard people say, "Oh, if only I had an extra $10,000, I'd be really happy." But those are the very people who remain dissatisfied when they get an additional $10,000.

If they had a million dollars more, they would not be happy, nor would they be successful.

Happiness is never the completion—the getting. Happiness comes from the work, the endeavor, the pursuit of a goal—the giving. Production, not consumption, is at the core of happiness and success.

If you can see progress in your work, then you will know happiness in that very process. Process is production, and production is giving. As Templeton is fond of saying, "Happiness pursued eludes, happiness given returns."

One way to understand happiness is to study happy people. Think of those you know or see who radiate happiness. What is the source of their joy? What lessons can you learn from them?

Templeton saw true happiness in the novices in Mother Teresa's order as they dedicated their lives to Jesus. As an investment counselor, he has considered it his business to closely observe his clients. Who is happy? Who is not? And what makes the happy ones happy?

His richest clients, he has come to realize, are not necessarily his happiest clients. He sees no clear correlation between wealth and happiness. It is not money alone that makes people happy. In gambling casinos, you rarely see anyone smiling, even those who have beaten the odds and are standing behind stacks of chips.

In fact, a sure system for understanding unhappiness is to assume the attitude of the gamblers in the casino. They have made the accumulation of money an end in itself, related to nothing but the turn of a card, the roll of the dice. If you do this, soon your own face will reflect the gambler's anxiety, unhappiness, and selfishness—even when beating the odds and winning large sums of money.

When you meet someone, always ask yourself this question: What makes him or her special? Look for the glow that person gives off, because everyone has a glow. There is a tendency to see only the faults in others. Obviously, all of us have personalities that are a mixture of good and bad elements, but if you form a habit of looking for the bad, then that's all you will see. If, instead, you train yourself to look for the good, you will find it. Seek out the good and your mind will fill with happiness. And happiness, being one of the purest forms of strength, is crucial to success.

Pleasing others is an avenue to happiness. If you please others, you please yourself. Early in his career, John Templeton learned that each client had to be treated differently. He worked diligently to answer the special wishes and needs and to solve the tax problems of each client. He asked a lot of questions; he listened carefully—he pleased. By pleasing others, he helped to fulfill himself. Today John Templeton has few individual clients; those individual accounts he does accept invest a minimum of $10 million.

Yet another success and happiness strategy is never to argue unless a useful purpose can be served. Too often we are ruled by our emotions. We start an argument without stopping to think of the consequences; nothing is achieved in the end except a mutual feeling of ill will. The proper tactic is to remain silent until you have determined that the disagreement will have positive results that can't be arrived at through reason and quiet discourse.

Once involved in debate, it is vital that you know your facts. Your argument should proceed from facts, not emotion. If you're well prepared, it's possible to disagree with someone in a way that is convincing and helpful to that person.

Templeton has sat in many board meetings, involving both large and small corporations, and he has carefully observed how directors behave in those settings. The successful directors (and the ones who run the most profitable companies) tend to be thoughtful and long-range in their thinking. When they raise a prickly issue, they will have the facts; they can prove why their way would bring better results. Poor leaders, on the other hand, will sometimes prove to be wrong after they have already lodged a complaint or an objection.

Know your facts. Speak only after you have thought. And hold your fire.

There are psychologists today who believe that anger

can play a positive role in our dealings with others. Experience with successful people, however, has convinced John Templeton that anger is a retrograde emotion that should be banished from our lives. It is not an intellectual pursuit. Basically, it unleashes destructive forces that cripple communication. Successful people think in terms of respect for others, not anger toward others. They reach out for accommodation rather than confrontation.

You should say to yourself, "Those people are doing what they believe is right. I don't have to agree with them, but there has to be a reason for their actions." Perhaps they recently received bad news. They may not be feeling well. The proper action is to answer their anger with love and logic.

Make them happy, not angry. Anger hurts no one more than the person entertaining it. It is a negative emotion that leads to unproductivity.

Jesus says, in the Gospel according to Saint Matthew (7:1–5): "Judge not, that you be not judged. For with the judgment you pronounce you will be judged, and the measure you give will be the measure you get. Why do you see the speck that is in your brother's eye, but do not notice the log that is in your own eye? Or how can you say to your brother, 'Let me take the speck out of your eye' when there is the log in your own eye? You hypocrite, first take the log out of your own eye, and then you will see clearly to take the speck out of your brother's eye."

John Templeton believes strongly that people should not

take others to court. He is in favor of settling problems short of litigation. The speck is in your neighbor's eye, the log is in yours, and two civilized people should be able to arrive at a peaceable solution.

Templeton says, "One of the things I have most pride in in my life is that I never sued anybody for anything, even though I've been the chief executive of literally dozens of corporations, including a group with as many as 500,000 shareholders. Nor have I, or any company controlled by me, ever been sued in my seventy-four years. I think that's a wonderful thing to try to achieve. In a way, it's a form of happiness.

"When I was a student at Yale, Professor Glenn Saxon, who taught industrial engineering, said we should try to solve problems by what he called integration. By integration he meant trying to understand the basic prevailing forces on both sides, rather than resorting to argument and name calling. If you can decipher those forces, you have a better chance of arriving at a solution that everyone can live with.

"You search for the underlying long-range motives on both sides and try to integrate them so that both parties can start working in the same direction."

We also achieve happiness by remaining active. Many people think of retirement as a blank page: nothing to do but sit around all day and be lazy. But if you want happiness, you must always have some project that you're working on. It's all right to end one career, providing that you have structured activities to fill the empty spaces. No matter what age you are—even if you're eighty, if you're ninety—you must continue to cultivate your talents.

Retirement works only if people plan carefully for it. It is good to set new goals for yourself, realistic goals. Often, if we think the future out in detail, the work we do after retirement can be more rewarding than the work we did all those years for a salary.

There are people who feel they're so old that they can no longer have useful goals. But that is rarely the case. For instance, if you are still able to write, you have a number of possible options. You can correspond with lonely people. You can work on your autobiography: We all have our own story to tell and no two stories are ever the same. You can write poems or short stories or novels and try to have them published.

John Templeton cites an example of how happiness and success can be achieved by the elderly. He had a roommate at Yale, John Bradley Greene, whose grandmother, Mrs. Talbot, was a wealthy woman.

She played no role in the business from which she drew a considerable income and could have simply done nothing. Instead, she undertook to help her children, grandchildren, and friends by seeking out inspirational articles, and once a year she would compile a calendar of 365 passages, one for each day of the year. Those people to whom she gave the calendar were uplifted by that day's inspiration. Her grandson at Yale shared those inspirations with young Templeton, who benefited from them in his life as an undergraduate, just as his friend's grandmother benefited by focusing her mind on a helpful and happy activity.

Perhaps Mother Teresa of Calcutta epitomizes better than anyone the concept that happiness can be achieved by what you do. She believes in showing love first to those who are near to you, those who cross your path every day. And that means even the panhandlers on the streets of American cities, even those who may use your money to buy a drink or drugs.

Mother Teresa explains, "Whenever we give, we give to Jesus. He has identified himself with the hungry, the naked, and the homeless to make it possible for us to love God. After all, how can we love God if not through others? Jesus has given us an opportunity to love God in action—through these poor who approach us for money in our cities, these poor to whom we already owe deep gratitude for accepting our services."

But what if a panhandler really does use his contribution to buy a drink or help pay for drugs? "I tell our sisters that I'd rather we made mistakes in kindness than work miracles in unkindness," she answers. "Maybe that man will buy a drink. Maybe he'll buy drugs. But then too, he may buy a piece of bread or pay for medicine for his child. We don't know. So I'd rather make a mistake than not to give at all. If someone approached me for something, I would always give it."

As John Templeton's spiritual sensitivities increased through the 1960s and early 1970s, he began to search for some significant, concrete way to spread the love and knowledge of God. The result was the Templeton Foundation Prize for Progress in Religion. It is annually awarded to an individual who has made a significant advance in any religion. It is the largest annual award given for any purpose.

The prize is a direct reflection of the personal values and religious views of Templeton himself. He decided it should be larger than any other prize in order to tell the world that progress in religion is more crucial than progress in any other area of life.

About 1970, Templeton talked with the British Governor-General of the Bahama Islands, Lord Thurlow, about the possibility of the queen of England awarding the Templeton Prizes just as the king of Sweden awards the Nobel Prizes. Lord Thurlow introduced Templeton to his friend, the Right Reverend Sir Robin Woods, Dean of Windsor. Sir Robin accepted Templeton's invitation to serve for three years on the original board of nine judges from all five major religions. He then talked with Prince Philip, the Duke of Edinburgh, who agreed to present the first award, to Mother Teresa of Calcutta, before an audience of 800 select guests in London's Guildhall. In fourteen subsequent years, the Templeton Foundation has invited Prince Philip to make the presentation and he has graciously accepted these invitations making the work of each prizewinner more widely known throughout the world.

When Mother Teresa traveled to London to receive the first Templeton Prize, reporters asked her why her nuns maintained a home there. They understood her need to remain near the destitute and dying in India, but what could she possibly accomplish in England's largest city, one of the main cradles of contemporary civilization?

She answered that her London house was one of her most important ones. She said that in London, as in all great cities, large numbers of people were starving and their condition was more serious than starvation from lack of food. They were starving spiritually. She explained that spiritual starvation was endemic among the wealthy, among those with an abundance of worldly possessions, and that her order's presence in London was meant to help such unfortunates.

There is a lesson to be learned from Mother Teresa about the true meaning of starvation. One of its dictionary definitions is "to be deprived of nourishment." If we are without goals, without God, without an experience and appreciation of our talents, then we cannot hope to find happiness. Success will elude us.

After reading Step 5, ask yourself the following questions:

1. Are you happier when you give a present than when you receive one?
2. Do you derive the most pleasure from activities that are geared to helping others or that add to their knowledge or pleasure?
3. Do you find that more differences are settled amicably through gentle persuasion than through angry confrontation?

4. Are you continually setting new goals for yourself?
5. Do you try to remain active throughout the day by pursuing a worthwhile activity?

If you have answered these questions in the affirmative, you are ready to proceed to Step 6.

STEP 6

FINDING THE POSITIVE IN EVERY NEGATIVE

A HIT SONG written by Johnny Mercer during the Second World War contained the words "accentuate the positive, eliminate the negative. . . . " For John Templeton they express one of his deepest beliefs: that you must be a positive person to succeed in life. Over the years he has compiled a list of quotations dealing with positive behavior, some of which might help those who tend to take the dark view.

Horace Rutledge, author of religious tracts, had this observation: "When you look at the world in a narrow way, how narrow it seems! When you look at it in a mean way, how mean it is! When you look at it selfishly, how selfish it is! But when you look at it in a broad, generous, friendly spirit, what wonderful people you find in it."

Lydia Maria Child, abolitionist and nineteenth-century author: "You find yourself refreshed by the presence of cheerful people. Why not make an earnest effort to confer that pleasure on others? Half the battle is gained if you never allow yourself to say anything gloomy."

Famous nineteenth-century English novelist George

Eliot had this to say on the subject: "Wear a smile and have friends; wear a scowl and have wrinkles. What do we live for if not to make the world less difficult for each other?"

French philosopher and mathematician Blaise Pascal put it this way: "Kind words do not cost much. They never blister the tongue or lips. Mental trouble was never known to arise from such quarters. Though they do not cost much yet they accomplish much. They make other people good-natured. They also produce their own image on men's souls, and a beautiful image it is."

Author J. Kenfield Morley put his views on a positive versus a negative viewpoint in the form of an aphorism: "I can complain because rosebushes have thorns or rejoice because thornbushes have roses. It's all how you look at it."

"A pessimist," said Reginald B. Mansell, a business executive, "is one who makes difficulties of his opportunities; an optimist is one who makes opportunities of his difficulties."

And, last, William Makepeace Thackeray, the author of *Vanity Fair*: "The world is a looking glass and gives back to every man the reflection of his own face. Frown at it and it will in turn look sourly upon you; laugh at it and with it and it is a jolly, kind companion."

Success depends to a very large extent upon enthusiasm. The Greek origin of the word *enthusiasm* means "in God." Therefore, the enthusiastic person is in tune with the infinite, with God himself.

Jesus said: "Beware of false prophets, who come to you in sheep's clothing but inwardly are ravenous wolves. You will know them by their fruits. Are grapes gathered from thorns, or figs from thistles? So every sound tree bears good fruit, but the bad tree bears evil fruit. A sound tree cannot bear evil fruit, nor can a bad tree bear good fruit. Every tree that does not bear good fruit is cut down and thrown into the fire. Thus you will know them by their fruits" (Matt. 7:15–20).

In business or socially or within your family, you will be known by your fruits. Love and joy—both positive emotions—are among the sweetest fruits of the spirit. God is the source of all love, and by tapping the divine source, you will radiate love and attract it at the same time.

You often come across people who say, "I can't find love anywhere." The reason they can't find love is that they don't give love. If you forget about trying to acquire love as though it's a material object that you can touch and, instead, concentrate on giving it, then love automatically comes your way. We must train ourselves to genuinely and deeply love every person; we will then, in return, be people who are magnets for love.

Remember: The ability to love without stint or qualification is a form of happiness. Happiness breeds success. And successful people are free to love.

God is an infinite source of love, and there is no limit to the amount of love you can get and give. All of God's love is ready to flow through you if you don't block it.

Think of yourself as a water faucet. If the faucet is on full, the water will flow through from the source and be a blessing to the person who drinks it or to the garden or flowers that need it. But if the faucet is turned off, no water flows and nothing grows.

There are those who think that smiling is facile and insincere. But you will discover that when you smile at someone who doesn't often show happiness, that person will immediately brighten. They have been waiting for the brightness that you shine on them, and they are ready to respond. Your face is a mirror that reflects happiness back onto others.

Another way to accentuate the positive is to welcome change each day. It is human nature to get stuck in a rut and resist innovation, but you must teach yourself to try new paths. Don't let a day go by without learning something new. The successful life is an adventurous one.

When John Templeton goes to restaurants with clients in connection with his investment counseling work, he makes it a point to order one item on the menu that he's never tried before. That way he assures himself that the day will not be like any other day; he assures himself of an adventure, a seminar in living, no matter how small.

A successful life depends less on how long you live than on how much you can pack into the time you have. If you can find a way to make every day an adventure—even if it's only a matter of walking down an unfamiliar street or ordering an untried cut of meat—you will find that your life becomes more productive, richer, and more interesting. You also become more interesting to others.

The same rule applies to travel. For example, make it your objective to visit all fifty states in the Union and at least a dozen other nations. You will thus have a positive goal worth pursuing and, as you begin to fulfill your goal, a sense of accomplishment. You will also begin to develop a worldview that will contribute to building a successful career.

So far, in his seventy-four years, John Templeton has visited forty-nine of the fifty states of the United States and seventy-seven nations in the world. He feels that extensive travel has enabled him to have viewpoints not obtainable to those who stay at home; he has also discovered wonderful new opportunities for investments.

To reach out, to try the new, is to accentuate the positive. The successful person never stops reaching and trying.

When Templeton first became an investment counselor after college, he had a friend, Harry J. Haas, a banker in Philadelphia. Haas formed a habit of making friends with other bankers whom he met at conventions and bankers' associations. He would write their names on individual cards and file them in his desk drawer. Subsequently, he would keep a sharp eye out for a photograph or any news item relating to them—a promotion mentioned in the business section of any newspaper, a recent entry in *Who's Who*, a social event—and whenever he found something, he would clip it out and attach it to the card. He collected cards on thousands of bankers, and he never failed to drop someone a line of congratulations on good news or commiseration if the news was bad. As a result, Haas, who through his thoughtfulness had made thousands of friends, later in life became president of the American Bankers' Association.

Men like Haas are uplifting forces in the lives of many. They make an extra effort to find the positive in every negative. Their genuine interest in others translates into substantial success.

John Templeton believes that we all have within us a deep reservoir of faith, but it often lies buried and unused. To bring it out takes training. You can teach yourself to talk to another person and glimpse that person's true faith. Every person has it, and if you can find it you will be able to genuinely express friendship, love, and joy—three great aids to becoming a successful and productive person.

If you meet someone at a party or in business about whom you can't find anything positive to say, it is best to say nothing. But if you can find something good to say, don't keep it to yourself. Pass on the good news to the person most eager to hear it—namely, that person. If, for example, someone has remarkably clear eyes, eyes that illuminate a room, compliment his eyes. If he has a soft and musical voice, tell him how pleasant it sounds. Whatever you find admirable about a person, let it be known. The telling also benefits the teller because the habit is established of expressing useful and constructive thoughts. The telling builds friendships. You have found the positive in the negative.

John Templeton gives an example from his own life of how positive behavior can draw family members together in a tighter, more loving bond. He says: "When my second wife, Irene, and I were first married, I had three young children and she had two. We wanted them to be friends, to feel like one family. So we decided to take them on an eight-week trip through Europe. That way, they would be together constantly, twenty-four hours a day.

"We found that we couldn't get all five children and us and our luggage in an automobile, and we realized that we'd have to buy a bus in Europe. So we invited three of my brother's children along for the eight weeks, making ten of us, eight children and two adults.

"Now, like many children, they wanted to have their own way about things. Right at the start, we made a crucial decision. We said, 'This is your trip. You're in charge.'

"In order to avoid any conflict, each child was given a particular responsibility and made the decisions in that area. The oldest girl was in charge of the money. The next oldest had to decide which cities we would visit and the hotels at which we would stay. Another was in charge of everything to do with eating. Another was responsible for the bus. One was in charge of photography. Another was the trip historian. Every second day, she would write about the most interesting thing that had happened to the group. We would then send her notes back to my secretary who typed them out, mimeographed them, and gave them to our friends as letters.

"The point is that we gave the children the authority. We gave ourselves only the hardest job, which was to keep our mouths shut when the young people made the inevitable hundreds of childish mistakes.

"Our duty was to get up each morning, pack our one bag each, sit down on the backseat of the bus, and then wait for the children to pay the hotel, tip everybody, and decide where to go next. And to keep our mouths firmly closed.

"The only serious mistake made all summer was not made by any of the children but by me. At the beginning of the trip, I handed out the cash for the first week to the girl in charge—all of it, rather than a portion—and it was more money than any of the eight children had ever seen before. They were overwhelmed by it and determined to manage it wisely so there would be plenty of money left over. I said they could divide any surplus among them, but there I made my mistake. They took such an interest in saving that they didn't want us to have a hotel room with a bath—too expensive. They were suddenly opposed to restaurants. They wanted us to buy food in grocery stores and eat on the bus.

"My son in charge of hotels, age seventeen, was the only one of the eight children who had been in Europe before, and he decided we wouldn't need any advance reservations. It happened to be the busiest tourist summer Europe had ever had up to that time, and here were ten of us in a bus with no reservations. We would drive into a town at about five o'clock in the afternoon and we'd say to my son, 'We're going to have tea while you find us a place to stay.'

"Surprisingly enough, he managed to find us a place to sleep every single night. Not always deluxe, but something.

In Yugoslavia we slept on cots in a high school auditorium, and in Frankfurt he came up with a restored bomb shelter with no windows.

"Like most children, the eight of them were prone to a certain amount of grumbling and squabbling. And there was one younger child in particular whose life was mainly one constant grumble. At the start of the trip we said to him, 'Your job is to police the attitudes of the others. If anybody says anything unpleasant, they must remain silent until they've found two happy things to say.'

"It worked like a charm. Not only did he conscientiously get on the others but, because he was the designated enforcer, he converted himself. The lively and warm side of his personality came out."

If complaints are invidious, so are comparisons, particularly comparisons between people. Almost every comparison is negative by its very nature. Rid yourself of the habit of saying, "This girl is prettier than that girl" or even "I like oranges better than apples." However they may be framed, comparisons have a negative aspect to them and are often harmful. The successful person learns to avoid comparisons of all types.

Instead, learn to say, "What a pretty girl!" or "I like oranges very much." The same ideas can be expressed without the use of comparisons.

John Templeton gives a dramatic example of how he learned this lesson: "As a young man I attended a house party. There was a girl there who wanted to know me better, and the host of the party had her listening in on our conversation while he asked me questions about her. I dealt in comparisons; I was carelessly negative, more than I meant to be. When later I discovered that she'd listened in, I was mortified. I was only trying to be honest and answer my friend truthfully, but I learned my lesson. Always talk as though the subject under discussion is an invisible presence who can see your expressions and hear every word you say. Then you'll be careful and scrupulous in your judgments. That's the kind of behavior that makes a successful person."

Gossip is another vice shunned by the success-bound person bent on finding the positive in the negative. Most gossip is adverse information, usually riddled with exaggeration and falsity. The individual who hopes to be successful, to be admired and popular in business, should work hard to avoid gossip.

The ability to speak well of others, without comparisons, and to avoid gossip are positive approaches to life. Most circumstances can be interpreted in two ways; it all depends on your point of view. When two people look at a given situation, one can take a positive posture, the other a negative one. There is the famous illustration of two people studying a glass of water. One says that it is half empty. To the other, it is half full. We can train ourselves to look up rather than down—by finding the positive in the negative, by viewing the glass as half full. Two guaranteed methods for approaching that happy state are to shun comparisons and avoid gossip in your relations with others.

John Templeton also recommends that you devote part of your reading time to material of an inspirational nature. *Guideposts*, a magazine with over 3 million subscribers, dedicates itself to uplifting stories. It forges a clear connection between business success and a life of inspiration.

Templeton recommends Norman Vincent Peale's books on the power of positive thinking; the television programs and books by Robert Schuller, featuring his method called Possibility Thinking; and the *Reader's Digest*. As Templeton points out, the inspirational movement is one of America's greatest success stories. *Reader's Digest* has become the most widely read magazine in the world, with the largest circulation, and has accomplished this without articles dealing with sensationalism, degradation, and violence. Reading inspirational material can be an essential item in yout success portfolio.

The motto of the Christophers, a Roman Catholic organization of hundreds of thousands of people, is that "it is better to light one candle than to curse the darkness." If you live by that precept, you will be following the steps to success.

Light a candle in the darkness that will illuminate your life and the lives of those around you, and that very light will lead you to your goal.

To summarize Step 6, anything that can be formulated in positive terms will lead to harmony among people and productive change. Through practice, you can almost always find the positive in any situation.

Below are listed areas for further study:

1. When you start to analyze the character of person B while talking to person A, stop yourself. Resist the impulse. It is gossip, and gossip is a negative force that leads away from success and happiness.
2. Avoid comparisons. They have a way of making negatives out of positives.
3. Be sure that your life is a seminar in living. You can achieve this by learning something new each day, no matter how small; by reaching out to others; by never passing up an opportunity for a new experience that will enlarge your knowledge; and by traveling as much as possible so that you can see new places and meet new people from different backgrounds.
4. Read literature that inspires you. Inspiration is a core characteristic of the positive personality.

STEP 7

INVESTING YOURSELF IN YOUR WORK

"I'LL BUY TWO Roman candles!" said one boy.

"Give me a pinwheel!" cried another.

"Three firecrackers for me!" demanded yet another.

Money was changing hands so fast that you might think an experienced adult entrepreneur was hawking fireworks for the Fourth of July. But such was not the case.

John Templeton, at the age of eight, was the salesman who had found the market and was busily raking in the profits. Even in those early days in his hometown of Winchester, Tennessee, he was beginning to make his mark in the world of business. And one of the most striking personal characteristics he displayed, while only a child, was the ability to formulate an idea, plan ahead carefully, and then invest himself totally in the work at hand.

How did hard work pay off for him at such a tender age?

Because there was no fireworks store in Winchester, there was a vacuum in the market and, hence, an opportunity for him. He did some research to see how he could buy quantities of fireworks at cut-rate prices and then sell them at a profit to his classmates. Through diligent detective work, he discovered a mail-order outlet in Ohio, and about a month before the holiday he was ordering various kinds of fireworks from Cincinnati—Roman candles, pinwheels, sparklers. You name it, he had it. Then, just before the Fourth, he would pack up his wares into his schoolbag, run off to class, and sell them to the other children at a healthy markup in price.

Young John Templeton had learned one of the cardinal success secrets at a tender age: the importance of hard work. In his long life, he has never stopped working hard, and he has never regretted a single moment of it.

Through his extensive reading, Templeton has compiled a number of quotations on the value of hard work and how hard work leads to success. Here are some of his favorites:

Chief Justice Charles Evans Hughes believed in "work, hard work, and long hours of work. Men do not break down from overwork, but from worry and dissipation."

The advice of Harlow Herbert Curtice, an automobile manufacturer, was to "do your job better each time. Do it better than anyone else can do it. Do it better than it needs to be done. Let no one or anything stand between you and the difficult task. I know this sounds old-fashioned. It is, but it has built the world."

Grenville Kleiser wrote some of the earliest successful "how-to" books. He believed that "there is honor in labor. Work is the medicine of the soul. It is more: It is your very life, without which you would amount to little."

William Feather, publisher and author, said: "The prizes

go to those who meet emergencies successfully. And the way to meet emergencies is to do each daily task the best we can; to act as though the eye of opportunity were always upon us. In the hundred-yard race the winner doesn't cross the tape line a dozen strides ahead of the field. He wins by inches. So we find it in ordinary business life. The big things that come our way are seldom the result of long thought or careful planning, but rather they are the fruit of seed planted in the daily routine of our work."

For Sir Theodore Martin, the nineteenth-century Scottish biographer: "Work is the true elixir of life. The busiest man is the happiest man. Excellence in any art or profession is attained only by hard and persistent work. Never believe that you are perfect. When a man imagines, even after years of striving, that he has attained perfection, his decline begins."

In the opinion of Thomas Carlyle, the Scottish essayist and historian: "The glory of a workman, still more of a master workman, that he does his work well, ought to be his most precious possession; like the honor of a soldier, dearer to him than life."

Henry Ford, the automotive great, believed that "nobody can think straight who does not work. Idleness warps the mind. Thinking without constructive action becomes a disease."

Author Jacob Korsaren gave this advice: "If you are poor, work. If you are burdened with seemingly unfair responsibilities, work. If you are happy, work. Idleness gives room for doubts and fear. If disappointments come, keep right on working. If sorrow overwhelms you and loved ones seem not true, work. If health is threatened, work. When faith falters and reason fails, just work. When dreams are shattered and hope seems dead, work. Work as if your life were in peril. It really is. No matter what ails you, work. Work faithfully—work with faith. Work is the greatest remedy available for both mental and physical afflictions."

The English statesman and man of letters Lord Chesterfield said: "It is an undoubted truth that the less one has to do, the less time one finds to do it in. One yawns, one procrastinates, one can do it when one will, and, therefore, one seldom does it at all; whereas, those who have a great deal of business must buckle to it; and then they always find time enough to do it."

Psychiatrist W. Beran Wolfe put it this way: "If you observe a really happy man, you will find him building a boat, writing a symphony, educating his son, growing double dahlias, or looking for dinosaur eggs in the Gobi desert. He will not be searching for happiness as if it were a collar button that had rolled under the radiator, striving for it as the goal itself. He will have become aware that he is happy in the course of living life twenty-four crowded hours of each day."

Former President Calvin Coolidge was certain that "all growth depends upon activity. There is no development physically or intellectually without effort, and effort means work. Work is not a curse; it is the prerogative of intelligence, the only means to manhood, and the measure of civilization."

And perhaps the Greek playwright Antiphanes summed it all up when he said: "Everything yields to diligence."

Very few of us work as hard as we can. We think we work hard. But in fact nine out of ten people waste more time than they use.

The successful person learns to avoid wasting precious moments. It is helpful to carry with you reading material that is necessary in your career. Then, when you have a few minutes between appointments or while riding on a bus or train, you can absorb a page or two, or an entire article. Thus you've used your time fruitfully.

Whenever possible, carry a tape recorder with you in your briefcase. You will find that you can jot down ideas and dictate letters, accomplishing something in what might otherwise be wasted time. Career success depends on such tactics. If you can learn to use all that time that would otherwise be wasted, you are learning the meaning of hard work.

Forty years ago, when John Templeton was first calling on investment counseling clients, he trained himself to arrive early for appointments. He set his watch ten minutes fast (he does to this day) so that he would be likely to be ahead of schedule at all times. While waiting for his appointment, he would spend those extra ten minutes reading.

Another way to save time is to think two thoughts at once, a trick that Templeton has mastered. He has found that it's possible while, say, giving a lecture to be thinking also of what you're going to do the next day. Our time is limited, and it's helpful to think along one channel while functioning on another.

As strange as it may seem, you will make fewer mistakes by distributing your thoughts over a wide range of consciousness and you will accomplish more. For example, if you're carrying on a conversation, analyze at the same time what your objective is in carrying on that particular conversation. Is it to produce a book or a paper? Is it to persuade someone? Is it to convey new ideas or to sharpen your own viewpoint through discussion?

Think while you talk. It takes long practice to train yourself to concentrate on a subject that you're not discussing or doing or reading about, but the payoff is that you can extend each workday by packing more substance into it.

Those who learn the secret of hard work will find success; the winning of awards and scholarships will point you in the right direction. The awards needn't be major; they can be ribbons awarded for winning a spelling bee or a swimming meet in school. But big or small, it pays to set yourself the task of winning an award because it trains you to work harder. Once you win something, you're all the more motivated to win something else.

We live in a credit economy and an advertising culture that advises us to buy now and pay later. At best this is a dubious proposition. The underlying philosophy—a dangerous one—is that we accept gratification before we've earned it.

Although it goes against the grain of our current "live for the moment" orientation, children should be taught to "study first and play later." If children do their homework in school or as soon as they get home, they will begin to build a reputation as students who know the meaning of responsibility and hard work. They will please their teachers, their parents, and themselves. They will make the honor roll and win scholarships. They will truly enjoy their leisure time because they will have earned it. Those children will already be on the fast track to success because they will have learned the first key lesson: Defer pleasure until the job is done.

When John Templeton worked for an oil company in Dallas, his first important position, he watched to see what time his boss arrived and left each day. Templeton then scheduled his time so that he was always in before the boss arrived and still at his desk when the man left each evening. He feels that his rapid rise had much to do with the impression he made on his boss as a man willing to work long hours. He was labeled as a hard worker, and hard workers advance the most rapidly in any enterprise.

It was in his second year at Yale, however, in 1931, that John Templeton truly learned the meaning of hard work. His father told him, "John, I can't give you one more dollar toward college. I can barely hold on through this depression."

The news was a blow to young Templeton's future hopes. But when he got over the initial shock, he searched for answers. Should he look for a job or return to college? He prayed and sought advice from family and friends. He mulled over their suggestions and offers, including that of his uncle, Watson G. Templeton, who was willing to lend him $200 if he would try to work his way through the next three years of college.

Templeton finally decided to borrow the money from his uncle. With a positive "can-do" attitude, he returned to Yale that fall prepared to scramble for the necessary funds to finish his education.

On his arrival, he immediately went to Ogden Miller, the man in charge of the college's Bureau of Appointments, and explained his financial predicament.

Because of his excellent freshman record, he not only received a scholarship but got employment from the university as well. He had taken a chance in returning to Yale on his uncle's modest loan. And now, to stack the odds solidly in his favor, he was forced to invest more of his own effort and sweat to see that the gamble paid off.

One lesson he learned during that period was that you must "always deliver more than you promise." Another lesson: "Seeming tragedy can be God's way of educating his children." Most important, the need to earn his own college expenses taught him the meaning of hard work and thrift.

Templeton says, "I knew that to continue at Yale I would have to get not one but several scholarships simultaneously. To do that I would have to have top grades, and so for the first time in my life, I became a really hard worker. Throughout my college career, I always had at least two scholarships, and at the end of my junior year, I was the number-one student in my class.

"How did this happen? Not because I was the smartest kid in my class. I wasn't. There were dozens of students with superior intellects. But I had learned to be a hard worker, and that's more significant in the end than being intellectual. Success depends more on how you develop your talents than on how many talents you have."

In college exams, you have to answer as many questions as possible as accurately as possible. One success secret that Templeton learned is not to dwell on those questions that pose difficulties. If you have an examination of ten questions, glance through it quickly and first complete the answers you are sure of. Do those accurately and thoroughly. Then try the others. If, by the time the examination is over, you have neglected anything, it is likely to be a question you couldn't have answered in any case.

Don't waste time on the impossible when you can make valuable headway in the area of the possible. That is a valuable success habit to carry through life.

John Templeton believes that successful people, ever conscious of time management, will not get their news from television. Too much time is wasted. During a thirty-minute program, there are numerous commercial interruptions and very little substantive news. For the hard worker, conscious of time, it is far more expedient to read a good newspaper. In only ten minutes with a newspaper, by running your eyes down the columns and picking out the headlines of significant items, then scanning what is pertinent, you will gain ten times the information you will receive from half an hour of television viewing. He further believes that no one who watches more than 100 hours of television a year will become a success.

Scanning is a must for anyone who hopes to be successful. There is far too much printed material in any given area for one person to digest in a single lifetime. You have to select whatever is most helpful. Proper scanning will allow you to increase your workload at least twofold. Also, proper scanning frees you from the drudgery of reading through long passages of material that aren't related to your interests. Skip items that are trivial and read those of lasting significance.

Because, as Korsaren said, "Work is the greatest remedy available for both mental and physical afflictions," in adversity it is important to work even harder, as Templeton did as a Yale sophomore. Too many people take the attitude that there are no suitable jobs for them. If these same people became givers rather than getters, they would move ahead much faster. They should ask themselves, "What can I give of myself and my talents that will please someone?" They should not simply say, "Give me a job with a salary."

This applies particularly to the sales area. Hundreds of corporations are delighted to have sales representatives if they can pay them on a commission basis. If you want to get started on the success course, you should carefully choose the industry with which you feel a kinship. You should then approach a company in that field and say, "Don't pay me anything. I'm not asking for a drawing account. Just let me sell your product." Then, once on board, it's up to you to give the job long hours and lots of enthusiasm. Remember, all the power of God within you is at work.

Margaret Thatcher has offered a program in Britain that would be worth considering in the United States. By offering a valid start-up plan, the unemployed there are provided money to go into business for themselves. So much is allotted to the person wanting to open a shoeshine stand; a larger sum goes to the person opening a restaurant at the seashore. If those recipients of government funds work hard and are successful, they hire others and thus the unemployment rolls are reduced even more. Of course, the plan's success—like that of almost every plan in life—depends on hard work.

Another key to success, and one that John Templeton recommends and tries to use himself, is to take one day off each week and use that time to do something that is both totally different and spiritually uplifting. Call it your sabbath day. It need not be a Saturday or a Sunday. Even those who are not churchgoers should observe a sabbath day, working on spiritual growth or charity.

As you climb toward success, striving each day and each hour to fulfill your goals, it is vital that you not neglect your sleep. John Templeton has worked long hours his entire life, putting in many fifteen-hour working days, six days a week.

Yet he has tried to get seven hours of sleep a night. Without proper rest, energy flags. In some respects, his approach to life, even at a young age, matched the method of time and energy management discovered by the hardworking founder of Methodism, John Wesley. At the age of eighty-five, Wesley wrote in his Journal:

> I this day enter on my eighty-fifth year; and what cause have I to praise God, as for a thousand spiritual blessings, so for bodily blessings also! . . . To what cause can I impute this, that I am as I am? First, doubtless, to the power of God, fitting me for the work to which I am called, as long as He pleases to continue me therein; and, next, subordinately to this, to the prayers of His children.
>
> May we not impute it as inferior means,
>
> 1. To my constant exercise and change of air?
> 2. To my never having lost a night's sleep, sick or well, at land or at sea, since I was born?
> 3. To my having slept at command so that whenever I feel myself almost worn out I call it and it comes, day or night?
> 4. To my having constantly, for about sixty years, risen at four in the morning?
> 5. To my constant preaching at five in the morning, for about fifty years?

6. To my having had so little pain in my life; and so little sorrow, or anxious care?

Like Wesley, John Templeton has possessed a positive, success-oriented, stress-conquering frame of mind. Also like Wesley, Templeton learned at an early age that regular sleep, rest, and relaxation were essential for him to maintain a high level of performance in all his tasks.

As a hard worker, you should form the habit of arriving at your office an hour early each day. Without telephone calls and other interruptions, you can accomplish in one hour what would take you two or three hours later in the day. Such early-bird behavior will help you to forge ahead in your career.

In conclusion, money earned through hard work is money with meaning. For many people—perhaps for most—easy money is poison. There is a universal tendency to say, "Oh, if only I had $100,000 I would be so happy." But if you study people who have amassed large sums of money easily, through gambling or winning the lottery or some fluke of fate, you will find that they are rarely satisfied.

The answer? Easy money and hard-earned money are different currencies. Individuals who have learned to invest themselves in their work are successful.

They have earned what they have. More than simply knowing the value of money, they know their own value. Those people are always the successful people.

Before moving on to Step 8, make certain that you have

absorbed the following points, which are indispensable as you climb toward success and happiness:

1. An idea is only an idea until you subject it to hard work.
2. Search for ways to turn problems into opportunities.
3. Work as if your life were in peril.
4. Carry your own library with you.
5. Think two thoughts at once.
6. Always go for the brass ring.
7. Defer pleasure until the job is done.
8. Build a reputation for delivering what you promised and, if possible, even more.

STEP 8

CREATING YOUR OWN LUCK

ON THE SUBJECT of luck, John Templeton has this to say: "There are many people who feel that success depends on the flip of a coin. And, of course, chance is involved in anything we do—things like timing enter in, for instance. But good luck always seems to arrive when you've worked hard and prepared for success. Without preparedness and plenty of sweat, luck is just a word with no real application to reality."

Templeton has a collection of favorite quotations on the meaning of luck, from which he feels the success searcher can profit.

Here's the view of Victor Cherbuliez, French novelist and literary critic: "What helps luck is a habit of watching for opportunities, of having a patient but restless mind, of sacrificing one's ease or vanity, of uniting a love of detail to foresight, and of passing through hard times bravely and cheerfully."

Philosopher Coleman Cox admitted: "I am a great believer in luck. The harder I work, the more of it I seem to have."

The American poet Walt Whitman wrote these lines: "There's a man in the world who is never turned down, wherever he chances to stray; he gets the glad hand in the populous town, or out where the farmers make hay; he's greeted with pleasure on deserts of sand, and deep in the aisles of the woods; wherever he goes there's a welcoming hand—he's the man who delivers the goods."

World-famous French chemist Louis Pasteur said: "Chance favors the prepared mind."

Author Max O'Dell gave his definition of luck: "[It] means the hardships and privations which you have not hesitated to endure, the long nights you have devoted to work. Luck means the appointments you have never failed to keep; the trains you have never failed to catch."

Psychiatrist Edward C. Simmons provided this definition: "The difference between failure and success is doing a thing nearly right and doing it exactly right."

Joseph Addison, the English poet and essayist, stated: "I never knew an early rising, hardworking, prudent man, careful of his earnings, and strictly honest, who complained of bad luck. A good character, good habits, and iron industry are impregnable to the assaults of all the ill luck that fools ever dreamed of."

And, last, in the immortal words of Branch Rickey, the baseball entrepreneur: "Luck is the residue of design."

To be a success, you have to understand that opportunity knocks only when—and if—you are searching for it. You can't just sit idly by and wait for "the lucky breaks."

John Templeton gives this example: "In studying bargains, it pays to inquire into the values of things and estimate their worth carefully—both present and future worth. I happen to know something about semiprecious stones, and once when I was in Rio de Janeiro, I stopped in a jewelry store and asked the prices of uncut amethysts, the crystals that they brought in from the mines.

"The store had a warehouse where they kept their uncut crystals. I persuaded them to drive me to the warehouse. I gazed at those beautiful objects, some of them as large as ten and twenty pounds. I asked the price; it was two dollars per pound and so I bought two tons of amethysts.

"Now I wouldn't have been able to do that if I hadn't prepared ahead of time. First, I had made myself knowledgeable enough to know that you couldn't go wrong with the crystals at that price. Second, I had been thrifty enough so that I had cash on hand for purchases when I found them.

"My company is still holding the crystals as a long-term investment. Having bought them in Brazil, I shipped them to a warehouse in Florida and they are there now. Eventually I'll sell them—and for many, many times what I paid for them. After all, God isn't making amethyst crystals very fast anymore."

What many people would call Templeton's "luck" in buying the uncut crystals that will one day bring him a small fortune is actually an example of how men like John Templeton make opportunities happen. They are always prepared, always alert to market changes and to the people who govern the markets.

The main ingredients of luck are hard work and proper

planning, along with the exercise of common sense and imagination. Perhaps the perfect example of how you make your own luck comes from John Templeton's early career as an investor. When Hitler invaded Poland in 1939, America had just gone through the worst depression in its history. There were more than a hundred companies whose shares had dropped below one dollar each on the New York and American stock exchanges.

But Templeton, at age twenty-six, was alert to a fundamental economic reality: In wartime there is great demand for so many kinds of products that even the inefficient companies can make a profit. Although the United States wasn't yet in the war, Templeton, who had done his homework carefully, was convinced that this country would be supplying the Allies and that we would most likely get involved in a direct way ourselves before too much time passed.

Translating these broad conclusions about the economy into practical reality, he decided in September 1939 to buy $100 worth of every stock on the exchanges that was selling for no more than a dollar per share. To finance the venture, he borrowed $10,000 from his employer.

At this point, it is important to note something about Templeton's philosophy of debt. Borrowing money for personal expenses—for paying for a vacation trip, for example—was anathema to him. This instance was different, however, because it involved a business venture in which the borrowed funds would be used to make money.

In other words, if he had borrowed for consumer purposes—say, to buy a new refrigerator or a car—the value of the object that he'd purchased would inevitably have depreciated. As a result, he would have had a debt to repay and no chance to make money from his purchase to cover that debt.

But, in borrowing money for business purposes, he was gambling that the profit from his investment would greatly exceed the principal and interest he would be paying on the $10,000 debt to his employer. This was, by the way, the only time in his entire professional career that he ever borrowed, even for business reasons.

There were two other factors that reduced the risk in the investment he was making. First of all, he had done thorough research during the previous two years on the performance of stocks selling for less than one dollar. And he had found that if their past records continued, it would be very unlikely that he would lose money. Second, through other wise investments and a stock-purchase plan he had with his company, his personal investment portfolio was now worth more than $30,000. So he had enough assets to cover the $10,000 he had borrowed if his theory proved wrong.

With this analysis firmly in place, he asked his former boss, Dick Piatt of Fenner & Beane, to place the order. Piatt said that the order was most unusual. He warned Templeton that he would do so reluctantly because thirty-seven of the companies on his list were in bankruptcy.

"That doesn't matter." Templeton told him. "Buy everything, whether it's in bankruptcy or not."

Many might call this a high-risk move, especially when

he was gambling with borrowed money. But he had done his homework well, as usual. He knew there was a chance that his scheme might fail, but he also knew that he had gathered the information and analyzed it as thoroughly as anyone could. His risk, in other words, was a reasonable one, with the odds stacked as much as possible in his favor.

The result? Of the 104 companies whose stock he had bought, only 4 turned out to be worthless. Within a year, young Templeton was able to pay back all the money he had borrowed. After he had sold all the stocks, an average of four years after he had bought them, his original $10,000 had swelled to $40,000. And there were those who called him lucky!

Templeton says of that experience: "I recall one stock in particular, a preferred stock of the Missouri Pacific Railroad. It had been issued in the 1920s to the public at a $100 a share, paying $7 a year cash dividend. But because of the depression, the company had gone into bankruptcy and stopped paying dividends. The shares went down in price until, at the time I placed the order, they were selling at twelve cents. So my one $100 bought 800 shares of Missouri Pacific Preferred.

"Then when we entered the war, railroads were needed. Missouri Pacific began to earn money again. The twelve-cent share shot up to $5 and I sold it, thinking I was wise. But as it turned out, I was only half wise. The price continued to climb until it reached $105 a share. So I sold too soon but, even so, I earned forty times my money.

"The moral is, don't enter into any business venture

unless, and until, you're fully prepared for it. I'm not aware of anyone else who did what I did. Not everyone had studied American stocks enough to realize why they were so cheap. Or perhaps no one had combined this knowledge with an analysis of wartime economics; therefore they didn't know that, in a major war, it's the most depressed companies that come back to life with the largest percentage gains."

Templeton has used his formidable knowledge, born of wide reading and research—some would call it his "luck"—in many other spectacular deals throughout his career. In 1985 an investor from New York who is an expert in Argentinian stocks observed to Templeton that because of Argentina's serious inflation and political instability, prices of their stocks were remarkably depressed. If their stocks were calculated in terms of American dollars, you could buy 100 percent of all the corporations listed on the Buenos Aires exchange for eight-tenths of a billion dollars.

Templeton knew immediately that the same computation for American stocks would be over $2 trillion—in other words, 2,500 times as much value. It was clear that the Argentinian stocks were absurdly underpriced. Within an hour, Templeton agreed to put up the capital, opened an account with a bank in Argentina, and bought $800,000 worth of Argentinian stocks at bargain prices. Within four months, prices rose 70 percent. Again, he was a big winner. A lucky winner?

In Matthew 7:7–8, Jesus says, "Ask, and it will be given you; seek, and you will find; knock, and it will be opened to you. For everyone who asks receives, and he who seeks finds, and to him who knocks it will be opened."

Asking means trying. It means giving your best effort under good as well as adverse circumstances. Seeking means using your facilities to the highest degree. If you seek, if you ask, if you try, if, most of all, you give all of yourself to any enterprise honestly and without stint or qualification, you are bound to have luck. You will find success.

Luck, in the final analysis, is what you make of all the options available. Always be prepared, make certain that your homework is done and that your ends are worthy, and the chances are you will be the luckiest of the lucky.

After completing Step 8, ask yourself these questions:

1. Do you believe in luck, and if you do, how would you define it?
2. Are you a lucky person? Luckier than most? Unluckier than most?
3. Would you agree that the person who works hard, intelligently, and creatively is bound to have more luck than the lazy and unimaginative person?

As you study Step 8, keep the following principles in mind. Luck will come to those who:

- Work hard and plan carefully.
- Are alert to opportunities.
- Use common sense and their creative imagination.
- Are willing to take calculated risks.

STEP 9

UTILIZING TWO PRINCIPLES OF SUCCESS

JOHN TEMPLETON believes that if you practice honesty and perseverance, the numbers will come up for you more than they do for the big lottery winners. Only your fortune will be based not on pure chance but on a solid foundation.

If there is a leading clue to Templeton's outstanding success, it is that he always finishes what he begins. He perseveres. Unfortunately, the world is full of people who start a project and then, as it presents difficulties, either postpone it or abandon it entirely. Thus they have gained nothing from the work they did.

Some people will even go so far as to finish 90 percent of a project and then, distracted, move on to something else. Try to train yourself not to commit to a project lightly; then, once committed, finish it! Excellent results and a solid reputation come from the follow-through.

When discussing perseverance, Templeton has a favorite saying: "The difficult we do immediately. The impossible may take a little longer." An exaggeration, of course, as he is the first to admit, but there is truth in the maxim nonetheless. When you undertake a project, don't be diverted, don't let yourself grow discouraged, but carry it through to completion and assume responsibility for your own results.

Templeton is fond of this quotation from the Swiss philosopher Henri Frederic Amiel: "He who floats with the current, who does not guide himself according to higher principles, who has no ideal, no convictions—such a man is a mere article of the world's furniture—a thing moved, instead of a living and moving being—an echo, not a voice."

Young Templeton's ability to guide his own life was put to a severe test on his very first paid job away from his hometown. For a shy young man, selling magazine subscriptions door-to-door was agonizing work. He felt totally unsuited and wanted to quit. But it was the summer before he was to enter Yale; he was seventeen and in real need of money.

Few people in 1930 had money to buy anything, let alone "extras" such as magazines. For that reason, selling magazines required more than just a hard sell; it required all the skills of persuasion and all the perseverance and patience one possessed. The sales supervisors even told the salesmen to run from house to house so they would seem breathless with excitement when they approached a prospect—just to make the sales impact greater.

For Templeton, it was a true test in perseverance. By temperament, he was all wrong for the job. He was uncomfortable in the role of salesman, and he considered the high-pressure methods unfair both to the customer and the salesman. But it was the only job he could find that summer. So he not only took the job but threw himself heart and soul into the challenge.

The company's policy was to give each salesman one dollar for each two-dollar subscription. And if a salesman happened to last through the entire summer and hit the 200-or-more subscription mark, he would receive a bonus of $200 over and above his commissions.

Templeton managed to stay the entire summer and he won the bonus as well. Perhaps equally as important, he learned the value of perseverance. He knew that once he had decided to sell magazines for the summer, he had to sell them as well as they could be sold. That meant putting his total self into the job; it meant being willing to make sacrifices, if necessary, to achieve his goals. It meant learning to persevere.

Perseverance in all of your daily activities leads to the formation of an orderly mind instead of one that is full of loose ends. It leads to a mind that is purposeful and capable of planning ahead. It leads ultimately to success in life because the habit of sticking to a given task, having now taken an interior form, helps you to convey facts more accurately and quickly.

If your thoughts are organized, you can explain more clearly to a customer the advantage of purchasing a particular stock. If you have an orderly mind, you can marshal your facts, present them with forceful logic, and persuade your client that one market position is superior to another.

The same principle applies to reporting to your boss. A young man in an automotive factory in China was interviewed by the Chinese leader Deng Zhao Ping, who was on a plant inspection tour. The leader listened intently to the young man's briefing and was so impressed with his clear and factual explanations that he promoted the worker to be his personal aide.

The moral? If you practice perseverance you will rise quickly. Perseverance will lead you to key people who can use you in their organization. It is a virtue that will make you an important person.

Persevering people will teach themselves to speak with economy, because they are the kind of people who persist at a given task and try to accomplish it with a minimum of waste. What we take a hundred words to say often may be said in ten well-chosen words. Practice paring down your speech. You will find that you are presenting your ideas more logically and that the information you convey is more accurate. You will be surprised, and pleased, at how attentively people listen to you when your delivery is crisp and to the point.

Pretend you are sending a cable; that is one of the best methods for learning economy of speech. Cables are charged for by the word. Soon you will eliminate extraneous clauses, unnecessary words, and other forms of fuzzy thinking. You'll begin to drive your points home with a force you never realized was within your power.

The persevering person will learn that in speaking and writing it is important to keep an outline in mind: This is idea 1, idea 2, idea 3, and this is the basic point I'm making. By using such a technique, you will be sure to present your ideas in a logical sequence. If you use the loose style of normal conversation, your audience will be left wondering what you were trying to say.

The outline approach is particularly useful when making business telephone calls. In the years when John Templeton was working eighty-four-hour weeks, he was dealing with literally hundreds of stockbrokers by telephone. The ones who said what they had to say succinctly and got off the line quickly were the ones he tended to call back. He knew that with them he wouldn't waste valuable time.

To persevere—to overcome opposition and fierce competition, both realities of the business life—you must use all the tools at your command. Templeton remembers one stockbroker, Norman Weiden, who made the telephone a brilliant success tool. "He got more of my business than anyone else," Templeton recalls, "because I could ask him a question on the phone and get back an answer within five seconds, and the answer was always on the mark. That efficiency made him valuable to me." Weiden eventually became a senior partner in one of the country's leading stockbrokerage firms.

Honesty and perseverance are the qualities you will find among the highest-caliber professionals. Always give your business to such people, regardless of the fee. You will learn from them and will receive superior service. Follow their example and you will become one of the highest-caliber professionals yourself.

Some people hire the lawyer who charges the least; that is a mistake. Chances are that in the long run it will cost you more. So whether you are dealing with a lawyer, doctor, or an accountant, find out who is the most knowledgeable, the most honest, and the hardest working, and you will find that is the one who will give you top service for your money.

John Templeton believes that his success in business is rooted in his honest relationship with his clients. He often quotes James F. Bell, a midwestern grain tycoon, who said: "Aside from the strictly moral standpoint, honesty is the best policy from the standpoint of business relations. The fulfillment of the pledged word is of equal necessity to the conduct of all business. If we expect and demand virtue and honor in others, the flame of both must burn brightly within ourselves and shed their light to illuminate the erstwhile dark corners of distrust and dishonesty. The truthful answer rests for the most part within ourselves, for like begets like. Honesty begets honesty; trust, trust; and so on through the whole category of desirable practices that govern and control the world's affairs."

John Templeton says: "I feel a strong duty to the 500,000 investors in our mutual funds. I consider it my duty—an act of faith—to see that their money is handled wisely. No matter what it costs, we try to seek out the best lawyers, accountants, and custodians for our business. And if we pay twice as much for their services than another company might consider sensible, they're still cheap—cheap because they do the job right.

"Because we have worked so hard to be faithful, honest, and responsible to our investors, and have put their financial well-being before all else, we have managed to create a superior record. For every dollar that an investor put in Templeton Growth Fund thirty-two years ago, he has eighty-two dollars today, if he reinvested all distributions.

"My favorite investor story has to do with Leroy Paslay, an old friend and a genius at electronic invention. We met many years ago when we both worked for an oil exploration company in Dallas. I thought so highly of him that we stayed in touch over the years. When I was ready to start the Templeton Growth Fund, I telephoned Roy and asked him if he would like to put some of his investments in a mutual fund. He said yes, he would put in $100,000, and he did. He has never taken a penny out. He has invested each distribution to buy more shares of stock. Today, he and his family have $8,200,000 in shares of this mutual fund.

"But nothing pleases me more than the attendance at our shareholders' meetings. In July of 1986, in Toronto, 1,400 people came from all over the world. I have never seen that many shareholders at a meeting of even the largest corporations. Maybe they come to us in such numbers because they trust us. Because we try to deliver good results consistently. Because we've worked for them honestly and have persevered on their behalf. Perhaps even because we start and end all of our meetings with prayer.

"We have never quit trying to improve our methods—and to provide our investors with high-quality service. The only success worth having, you know, is success that reaches out and touches others."

Honesty and perseverance—if, like John Templeton, you try to follow these two principles of success, you will be investing wisely in your own development. And you will find that others will want to invest in you.

To summarize Step 9:

1. Successful people finish what they begin. Be sure to think carefully before you take on a task, but, once you start it, complete it with thoroughness, energy, and resolve.
2. Handle all of your business relationships—and particularly other people's money—as a sacred trust.

Before going on to Step 10, ask yourself these questions:

- ▷ When you are hired to do a job, do you give it your all?
- ▷ Do you avoid cutting corners and give as much as promised or even more?
- ▷ Do you accept each assignment as a fresh challenge and a chance to grow in your profession and as a person?

If you are able to answer yes to these three questions, or can spot your weak areas and are ready to improve on them, you are ready to proceed to Step 10.

STEP 10

MAKING TIME YOUR SERVANT

THERE IS AN old saying in the U.S. Navy, "Loyalty up and loyalty down." The same principle applies to all the steps to success, including the ability to be the master of time and not its slave. There are people who will make a point of being prompt with their bosses but keep their own assistants waiting. But promptness with everyone, regardless of rank, and on all occasions, is a prerequisite of success.

Promptness is putting the others first. It tells others that you have regard for them, that you refuse to waste their time.

Nothing will impress your boss more than promptness. John Templeton, who has served as the chief executive of many corporations, looks above all for a job done correctly and on time. If you are asked to deliver a report at noon on Friday and you deliver the results at noon on Friday, you are bound to get ahead.

Some people, given that same job, will let it slide a little. Friday noon will come and go. They will wait a day or two, or a month. Or forever. But the people who time and time again deliver their assignments promptly are the ones who will forge ahead.

Many important people have been involved in the Templeton Foundation Prize for Progress in Religion. Templeton says: "It has been our practice from the beginning that anyone who participates in a charity program will receive a thank-you letter within twenty-four hours of the time they helped us. You don't wait a month, or even a week. You thank the person right away. In this case, we have letters prepared, and as soon as they've finished their part of the ceremony a messenger dispatches notes of thanks to them.

"Promptness is politeness and consideration. It's also good business."

Success-bound people learn early in their careers to avoid procrastination. Too many people have what could be called a *mañana* attitude. Why do it now? Tomorrow is soon enough. And the job is shunted off the main track—not necessarily until tomorrow either, as *mañana* would suggest, but to some future time, who knows how far away. Someone once said, "I'm going to conquer this problem of procrastination. I just keep putting off getting started."

Those afflicted with the procrastination habit are never likely to be successful. Who wants to deal with anyone, or rely on anyone, who suffers from the *mañana* disease?

Nothing is truer than the old saying, "Never put off until tomorrow what you can do today." If it is possible to do it today, do it today. Squeeze all that you can into today's schedule.

Only once in John Templeton's seventeen-year school career did anyone ask him if he'd done his homework assignment. Because young Templeton found Latin a difficult subject, his mother, who had studied Latin for seven years, would sometimes help him. She once asked him if he'd finished his work. He hesitated but finally told her: "Mother, all my life I've gotten nothing but As. Even in Latin. Not a single grade lower than an A. So please leave it up to me. I love you for your solicitude, but you needn't worry." She never asked him again.

John Templeton understood the virtues of promptness and stick-to-itiveness at a tender age. When he was in the first grade, he took his report card home and showed his father, with understandable pride, that all of the subjects were marked A. His father was very pleased and said that he would like to set up a contest. On each of John's half-year reports that showed nothing lower than an A, he would give his son a bale of cotton. Each time there was a grade lower than an A, however, John would have to give his father a bale of cotton.

The theory was that son would wind up owing father many, many bales of cotton, which would be a lesson to John. But the older Templeton did not reckon with his son's willpower, desire to succeed, and his early ability to get the most out of the minutes in an hour. He worked hard at his lessons, he was always prompt with them, and he went through grammar school and high school without a single grade below an A. Thus, eleven years later, his father owed him twenty-two bales of cotton.

John Templeton says, "Promptness in business is a must.

We manage six large mutual funds and have over 300 stocks and bonds in those funds. They are in more than twelve nations. And yet, within one hour from the close of the New York Stock Exchange, every last item we manage is priced worldwide and multiplied by the number of shares; all the dividends and distributions are calculated. We know in less than an hour the exact price to the penny of our stock so that those results can be published in the financial sections of newspapers.

"I can think of no better way to operate than to do now what should be done now. It is a hard way, but the best way, and a useful principle for success."

There are two quotations on the virtues of promptness that John Templeton feels will aid the reader searching for success.

The first is from William Mathews, the philanthropist: "Nothing inspires confidence in a businessman sooner than punctuality, nor is there any habit which sooner saps his reputation than that of being always behind time."

The second, from author Sir Richard Tangye: "During a very busy life I have often been asked, 'How did you manage to do it all?' The answer is very simple: It is because I did everything promptly. Tomorrow is never. Yesterday is gone. The only moment is now."

Step 10 deals with the difficult subject of time management. Answer the following yes-or-no questions:

1. Are you the master of time and not its slave?
2. Do you manage your schedule so that you don't have to rush—and risk carelessness—to be on time?
3. Are you equally prompt with your superiors, your peers, and those who work under you?
4. Do you set your watch ahead in order to be prompt for appointments?
5. When you are given an assignment, do you complete it when requested or even ahead of time?

If you cannot answer yes in all five cases, go back to Step 10 and read it over carefully. Be sure to set your watch ahead. Keep a chart of appointments and activities hour by hour, and write out a list of tomorrow's engagements today. Before long you will begin to master the all-important art of promptness.

STEP 11

GIVING THE EXTRA OUNCE

EVEN AS A BOY, John Templeton was an observer of people. He watched them in every phase of their lives, studied them, and questioned why they did certain things—and what impact those things had on their happiness and level of success. He was strongly impressed by the discovery that the moderately successful person did nearly as much work as the outstandingly successful one. The difference in effort was quite small—only an "extra ounce." But the results, in terms of accomplishment and the quality of the achievement, were often dramatic.

Templeton called this principle the "doctrine of the extra ounce." And he quickly noticed that the doctrine was confined not to just one field of endeavor but could be applied in all fields. In fact, it seemed to be a kind of universal principle that could lead to success in life.

For example, when it came to high school football games, Templeton discovered that the boys who tried a little harder and practiced a little more became the stars. They contributed the key plays that won games. They tended to be the ones who gained the support of the fans and were complimented by the coaches. And all because they did just a little bit more than their teammates.

Templeton also noticed that same doctrine of the extra ounce at work in his high school classrooms. Those who did their lessons reasonably well received good grades. But those who did their lessons a little bit better than anyone else—who exerted the "extra ounce"—received top grades and all the honors.

The same principle applied to his experiences at Yale. Templeton made sure that he had his lessons not just 95 percent right but 99 percent right. The result? He got into Phi Beta Kappa in his junior year and was elected president of the Yale chapter—an accomplishment that went a long way toward helping him be selected for a Rhodes scholarship.

Out in the business world, Templeton refined his doctrine of the extra ounce even further. He came to realize that giving that single extra ounce results in better quality. Those who try harder are capable of a higher level of performance. And the person who gives seventeen ounces to the pint rather than sixteen will achieve rewards all out of proportion to that one ounce.

John Templeton's doctrine of the extra ounce is particularly noticeable in professional sports. Some will give their very heart and soul on the baseball diamond, and they are highly rewarded for their supreme efforts. Pete Rose is a perfect example. He may not have been the most talented player on the field, but his genius lay in giving top quality day in and day out for more than twenty years. He has never given less than his total ability.

The same principle applies in the music world.

How many musicians are world famous? How many are wealthy? What is the difference between those chosen few and other musicians?

The answer? That tiny bit extra. The giving of that additional ounce—that seventeenth magical ounce—that, for those who can force themselves to give it, pays off a thousandfold.

Not only does this principle apply in art but in the world of business, too. In the mutual fund field, where John Templeton has made a mark beyond most other men, you can get by with a performance that is slightly above average. Get by, yes, but you won't attract much attention. You will never enjoy the fruits of major success. If, however, you're willing to give that extra ounce so that occasionally you have the top performance of all the mutual funds, then you attract a huge following and become a leader in the industry.

Even the overachievers, though, must follow certain rules. First of all, when you promise a result, make sure it's realistic and that you can deliver. Even better, give more than you promised. This is especially true in managing corporations that are involved in long-range planning. If you are constructing a building or an airplane, you are going to have a budget extending two or three years or even more into the future. A budget is a powerful kind of promise. If your work comes in ahead of schedule and below budget, you've exceeded your promise. Then, on top of that, if your work is of the highest quality because you gave the extra ounce, you are a prime candidate to move ahead in your company.

Always underestimate what you can accomplish; this is a key success tactic. There is a temptation among ambitious executives to overstate their abilities and what they can produce. Even in risk situations, they will say, "Don't worry. I will have this done in such and such a time."

If there is any doubt in your mind, refrain from grandiose promises. Present the case factually and your ability to handle it realistically. Then work as hard as humanly possible to better your promise.

If someone asks you what you can do for them that John Doe can't do, give a careful and reasoned answer. Big words, brag words, can come back to haunt you. Don't say you'll produce 15 percent a year in your mutual funds. Say, instead, that you will do everything within your power to produce a superior result. If you then do more than promised, everyone is happy. But if you make exaggerated claims, you will create a group of discontented clients, and that can hurt your career.

To put this problem in another context, we all know people who brag constantly. Every reader of this book has at least one such acquaintance. Their bragging soon takes the form of unrealistic claims and promises; they will tend to rush projects, thus producing inferior quality. Such people soon earn a reputation for unreliability. Destructive self-inflation has ruined many a promising career.

The secret to better quality is to never give less than your best—to give that extra ounce. Although you should be careful not to undertake more tasks than you can handle, commit yourself totally to those that you do take on. Work at them until you are satisfied. It is safe to assume that if you are honestly happy with your results, your customer or employer will be equally as happy.

Templeton believes that better quality and lower cost—fruits of giving the extra ounce—are fundamental principles of Christianity. The Bible teaches you to develop your talents to the utmost. Thus, promising what you can realistically accomplish and then delivering it are true ministries.

As an investment counselor, Templeton has found that it pays to search through thousands of corporations to discover which is the lowest-cost producer of each item. If you are going to select successful investments, you should study and analyze the available information. That way, you can be confident that a certain steel company in South Korea, for example, is the world's lowest-cost producer of steel and that the sugar industry in Cuba is the world's lowest-cost producer of sugar.

If you fail to gather your data, you can't make an accurate assessment of which companies are likely to forge ahead, which companies are going to survive in periods of business depression, which companies are prepared to give better quality. And that is the kind of information—garnered through the doctrine of the extra ounce combined with solid preplanning—that leads to success, both for yourself and your clients.

To make others believers in giving the extra ounce and producing better quality, it's imperative that you have high team morale. Your staff must be motivated to work together with pleasure and enthusiasm. Contrary to the popular romantic notions about business, the successful executive is not a loner. Give credit and praise to others. Be quick to point out how much help you've received from others and what a central role they have played in your accomplishments. Whenever any praise comes to you, that praise is due to all of your fellow associates. Make sure you're right down in the trenches with them at all times.

In order to promote an attitude of the extra ounce, it has been John Templeton's practice for more than thirty years to pay employees about 20 percent above the current trade salary levels. That is not the result of kindheartedness, Templeton is quick to point out. Rather, it is his belief that if you pay 20 percent more than normal, you will gradually accumulate a superior team; for 20 percent more money, you will field a team that is 50 percent more effective. "You get what you pay for," Templeton says. "The old adage is true."

However, there are times when you will make an error in judgment; you will find that some people on your team do not pull their own weight. In such cases, Templeton does not recommend that you adopt the charitable view and swallow your mistake, nor does he believe in taking a cutthroat, unloving attitude. Once having admitted the mistake, you should try to find an area in which those employees are proficient and shift them into it. If you can't find such a spot in your own organization, find it in someone else's. Then you can go to the employees and explain that while what they are doing presently is neither to their own or the company's advantage, you have found a slot for them where they have a chance to become important and successful people.

Templeton is a great believer in the Japanese philosophy of management. Their companies study each employee as though he or she was a family member. They want to know where their employees' talents lie, where they will be the most productive. If they are no longer needed in one area, the Japanese company will shift them to another division, or into one of their associated companies. If a place can't be found for them anywhere in the organization, they try to retrain them for something they can work at until retirement age.

Templeton feels that the Japanese way is both intelligent and deeply ethical. They know how to get the extra ounce from their workers. He says: "I advocate the Japanese viewpoint wholeheartedly. By taking care of your employees, they will be devoted. They will work harder. The quality of the product will be superior. But what is especially striking about their method is the commitment and loyalty involved.

"Think of it in these terms. When you get married, you know your spouse won't always be young. He or she may have problems later in life, but problems don't end your responsibility. It's the same way with your employees. They may give you valuable service for years and then, for a vast range of reasons, they may run into roadblocks. But your responsibility to them must remain steadfast. If you don't give up on them, they will find a way to repay you with quality performance."

They will repay you by giving you that magical extra ounce.

To summarize Step 11, you should absorb the following lessons on the road to success and happiness:

1. To be outstandingly successful you must work just a little harder than those who are moderately successful. Learn to give one extra ounce and your rewards will be all out of proportion to that ounce.
2. The extra ounce results in producing higher quality in all lines of work.
3. If you give the extra ounce, your morale will be high and the teamwork you can achieve with fellow workers is bound to be extraordinary.

As you study Step 11, ask yourself this simple, two-part question. Consider it from as many angles as possible and answer it as honestly as you can: Am I giving all that I'm capable of, or is there an ounce of effort that I've withheld?

STEP 12

CONSERVING YOUR RESOURCES TO BEST ADVANTAGE

When John Templeton and his first wife, Dudley, got married, they made, along with the usual resolutions, a private pledge to put aside 50 percent of their total earnings for a personal investment portfolio.

For a full understanding of such a commitment to thrift, it helps to look again at Templeton's Tennessee boyhood. In his hometown of Winchester, the honor and character of people were their greatest sources of wealth. And one of the major marks of character was thrift. People who didn't save something—at least a few dollars of their weekly paycheck—were considered undisciplined and weak.

Thrifty people, on the other hand, were respected. So from the time he was young, Templeton learned that thrift was a character trait well worth developing. After the economic crash of 1929 the importance of thrift assumed a life-and-death significance. The 1930s gave ample evidence that to survive and prosper one had better save money and invest it wisely. Quite simply, conserving your resources to best advantage was essential to success and security. Those who saved received great rewards. Those who didn't went under.

As tough as the times were, Templeton and his young wife stuck by their decision to set aside fifty cents of every dollar earned. It wasn't an easy decision to carry out; it took willpower, perseverance, and total commitment to the future. It took the very qualities that spell success.

To make the personal sacrifices more tolerable in the early years, the young couple created a game out of being thrifty. And friends and neighbors often helped them realize their highly unusual financial venture. For example, friends found restaurants for them where they could eat a full, wholesome dinner for fifty cents. This was, of course, during the depression years.

Furthermore, Templeton never paid more than $100 a month for rent. He set a goal that rent would not exceed 16 percent of annual "spendable income," defined as the money left over after taxes, savings, and investments. And he became so adept at finding bargain-basement housing that rarely was that percentage even approached.

The Templetons had no need for luxury, for posh surroundings. They could get along happily without them. They had something better—a vision, a goal.

Thrift was like a light shining on the path that would lead them into a successful future. For twenty-five dollars they furnished a five-room apartment. That feat—astonishing even for the impoverished 1930s—was accomplished by going to auctions and bidding on pieces of secondhand furniture when no one else offered a competing bid. As a result, at one auction Templeton bought a bed for one dollar and a sofa for five dollars.

Anything not available at flea markets or auctions, Templeton constructed from wooden boxes. The result, of course, was hardly high elegance. As one friend put it, "'Early attic' was the basic style of the place."

But their living quarters during those years were always warm and comfortable, mainly because of their shared long-term goals. Their pronounced thriftiness was more an adventure than a burden because they believed profoundly in what they were doing. They had a definite objective toward which they were saving—complete financial security—and they never for a moment lost sight of it.

The fact is, however, that John Templeton was not poor even then. He had a good income and a solid investment portfolio that was steadily growing. Some acquaintances might have regarded his approach to money, housing, and the conveniences of life as somewhat eccentric, if not socially unacceptable. After all, the circles that Templeton, the investment counselor, frequented were characterized by big money, big houses, big cars, and big consumer spending in general. But Templeton was not one to live by society's more superficial values. He followed his own inner dictates and his developing religious beliefs.

And so a radical philosophy of thrift became a deeply rooted part of Templeton's way of life. He became convinced that success was closely connected to saving, a belief that he has never stopped practicing.

John D. Rockefeller often spoke of what he called "the magic of compound interest," a magic that anyone can practice so long as he first practices thrift. Although it may not at first seem there would be a big difference between investments that earned 15 percent per year instead of 12 percent, the facts are truly startling. Over a sixty-year period, each dollar at 12 percent would grow to $900, while each dollar invested at 15 percent would grow to $4,400!

To take advantage of compound interest, you have to be thrifty. You must be prepared, by virtue of careful financial management, to leave your money invested and let it grow. Then the magic, and the success that goes with it, can be yours.

Sometimes it is wise to borrow in order to build a productive asset that shows great profit potential, but, in general, heavy borrowing is unwise. In Templeton's investment work, he has found that most companies without debt are able to ride through the stormiest economic cycles without trouble. However, the companies with high debt—even though, in other respects, they may be equally good—may sink because they can't meet their obligations.

The horrors of debt were made obvious to John Templeton when he was still in high school. A friend of his worked for a dollar a day, six days a week, and on Saturday he would be paid six dollars. But time and again, he would borrow four dollars from young Templeton on Thursday by promising him his entire paycheck of six dollars on Saturday. In other words, he was so unthrifty that he couldn't manage for two additional days and resorted to selling six dollars for four.

Templeton calculated the rate of interest his unfortunate friend was paying. It opened his eyes to the ways people could ruin their lives. It is best never to borrow—not even money to buy a home—and he rarely did. The two exceptions were the $200 he borrowed from an uncle to help finance his college education and the $10,000 to get him started in the investment business. They were exceptions to his general rule and in neither case did he borrow for a strictly personal expenditure.

One of the best examples of how deeply the trait of thrift is embedded in John Templeton's character involves two cars. When barely a teenager, he was playing with friends in a hay barn about a mile from his house. During the horseplay he stumbled upon an old, broken-down Ford.

In a flash of insight about what that decrepit vehicle could mean to him and his friends, he approached the farmer who owned the barn and asked, "Do you want to sell that car?" The farmer answered that John could have it for ten dollars.

So John went home, withdrew some of his savings, explained the situation to his always supportive mother, and the car was his. That part went easily. The hard part was finding another Ford that could be used for parts to get the first one in working order.

So John searched all over the county for a second Ford that was the same make and model as the first. Finally, due to his persistence and a natural flair for ferreting out the best bargain, he did find the matching Ford. If possible, it was in even worse condition than the one he already owned, but it had the same virtue—it only cost ten dollars.

Some people might have scoffed that he was wasting his money by sinking it into two broken-down automobiles. But the scoffers didn't know that he had a plan—a plan that he was confident would turn two useless cars into one reasonably functioning motor vehicle.

With his equipment and parts assembled and tools borrowed from his brother Harvey, young Templeton and his eighth-grade friends moved to stage 2 of their plan—transferring the parts from one of the cars into the other.

They never lacked confidence that they were smart enough to put a car together. Nor were they lacking in youthful enthusiasm and energy. If they got stuck in their effort to assemble a workable jalopy, they ran down to the local Ford dealer and pored over his repair manuals until they were clear on the principles to follow. They got to know the mechanics around Winchester and picked up valuable tips to help them complete their project.

After nearly half a year of working afternoons and weekends, Templeton and his friends finally got one of the cars to run. They painted it orange and green and named it Esmeralda. And, surprisingly, with the help of constant and careful maintenance, the car they had rebuilt performed for four straight years, long enough to get the boys to and from classes and to out-of-town ball games in style until they graduated from high school.

John, always aware of the importance of thrift, had recognized a bargain in those two cars and, with the help of his friends, had turned his dream into a reality, for only a twenty-dollar investment. As a matter of fact, the first five cars owned by Templeton were secondhand and none cost over $200. He never paid more for an automobile until his net worth exceeded $250,000.

In 1940, when Templeton opened his office as an independent investment counselor, one of his first priorities was to acquire a reference library. As he researched the problem, he discovered that Fenner & Beane, for whom he had once worked, no longer had need of their library as they had merged with Merrill Lynch. Templeton went to the man in charge of moving and offered him twenty dollars for the research material, including twelve excellent bookcases. His offer was accepted. Any one of the bookcases would have cost $100 new, but Templeton caught his old company in the midst of a move when bargaining for unneeded books and furniture had no priority. Thus, by searching carefully for the best bargain, Templeton bought himself a library that he used for twenty years. All for twenty dollars!

John Templeton loves to quote Charles Dickens's Mr. Micawber on the subject of thrift: "Annual income twenty pounds, annual expenditure nineteen ninety-six, result happiness. Annual income twenty pounds, annual expenditure twenty pounds ought and six, result misery." To Templeton, that observation is at the heart of the difference between those bound for success and those who will flounder and perhaps never find their way.

Also, there is the story told about Prime Minister Disraeli that Templeton finds both amusing and edifying. Disraeli was taking a horse-drawn taxi in London, and when he reached his destination, he tipped the driver a shilling. The man said, "But sir, I often drive your son and he always tips me half a crown."

Disraeli answered, "Yes, I can understand that easily. You see, he's the son of a rich man."

But Templeton's favorite story involving thrift and the miracle of compound interest is the sale of Manhattan by the Indians to the Dutch for beads worth twenty-four dollars. "In history we're taught that the Indians were foolish to sell Manhattan for so little," Templeton says. "But if you look at the reality of compound interest you'll find that if the Indians had invested their money at 8 percent interest at the time of the sale, they would now have $11 trillion. That is more than the value of all the real estate in the entire Western Hemisphere today!"

There are other thrift habits and tactics that will lead to success. From the time Templeton began to support himself at eighteen until he was wealthy enough to move to Nassau in the Bahamas more than thirty years later, he never had a charge account. He never had a credit card. He never carried a mortgage. He never paid more than one year's income for the entire cost of a house. (He could remember clearly from his childhood in Franklin County, Tennessee, that people who had mortgages on their property were at great risk.) Even today, he travels only in an airline's economy class and enjoys giving the saving to charity.

When Templeton opened his investment counsel office in the RCA Building in New York's Radio City in 1940, he told his secretary never to buy a new typewriter. The value of typewriters declines 30 to 40 percent the day they leave the store. They bought reliable, secondhand machines, most of them no more than a few months old, for an average of 40 percent below retail price.

The typewriter principle, Templeton reasoned, could be applied to office space. He didn't need to spend on show, on something glittery and new. He simply needed the right amount of room in which to function.

When he found that he'd outgrown his space in the RCA Building, he decided that it would be more economical to have the research department near his home in Englewood, New Jersey. He found space in an old building above a drugstore, and because it was in disrepair, he was able to rent it for one dollar per square foot per year. Templeton spent a few hundred dollars fixing up the entrance to lend it an air of dignity. And, most important, he had over 2,000 square feet of office space for $2,000 a year.

Because of his devotion to thrift—in small items like typewriters as well as large ones like office space—after the first two years John Templeton's corporation operated at a profit every year.

Templeton believes that a central key to thrift is to become self-supporting at an early age. Only when responsible for their own expenses will young people become thrifty and mature enough to be capable of running businesses of their own.

In the rural South where John grew up, there was a tradition that the children would support their parents when the parents became sixty years old. Templeton feels that was a great help to both generations. The young developed character and a purpose beyond themselves, while those growing old were finally relieved of their harshest financial burdens. Grandparents living with children and grandchildren were happier than those living alone and were also helpful in rearing the grandchildren.

The Japanese today follow a similar model. The oldest son knows that it is his duty throughout life to support his parents when there is need.

Templeton learned many of his lessons of conserving his resources from the farmers of his youth. He observed them carefully. Most who got into trouble owed money. Those who didn't, didn't. It was as simple as that. Throughout extended depressions, lasting as long as six or eight years, those farmers free of debt could reduce their consumption and continue to live on their farms and not fear losing them. But those who had borrowed saw their debts skyrocket.

Eventually many lost their farms to pay off their debts and were without a place to live.

The principle that Templeton learned from watching the Tennessee farmers carried over to the stock market. There were far too many people who had bought their stock on margin. Those people were wiped out. When the prices went down, they had no more cash to put up and the brokers were obligated to sell them out. Of course they were forced to sell at precisely the wrong time, when stocks were depressed far below their real value. But those who had no debt and had refused to buy on margin rode out the depression with no permanent damage. Again, thrift was the saving factor. Thrift paved the way to success.

What applies to farmers and stock-market investors also applies to the oil industry. In the 1920s there was a boom in oil drilling. Many people borrowed heavily to drill. Others used their own hard-earned savings. Then, when the East Texas fields came in with huge production, the price of oil dropped to ten cents a barrel. Those producers who had borrowed heavily couldn't meet their debts and lost their oil leases. But the thrifty ones were able to live through what proved to be only a few difficult months until the price of oil recovered to about a dollar a barrel.

Observing those grassroots economic lessons wasn't the sum total of John Templeton's education in the use and misuse of money. He also read and studied the lives of Benjamin Franklin, John D. Rockefeller, and others. He took to heart what Rockefeller said about wealth: "If you want to become really wealthy, you must have your money work for you. The amount you get paid for your personal effort is relatively small compared with the amount you can earn by having your money make money."

> Neither a borrower nor a lender be; For loan oft loses both itself and friend, And borrowing dulls the edge of husbandry.

Those words of Shakespeare have meant a great deal to John Templeton. He has lived by them. He has grown to great success, both inwardly and in worldly terms, by observing and honoring their sentiments. He has made his own financial base secure—in fact, virtually impregnable—by avoiding all consumer debt.

You can do the same. To paraphrase Mr. Micawber: If you earn a dollar and spend a dollar ten, you'll be a failure. But if you earn a dollar and spend ninety cents, you're on the road to success!

As Step 12 makes clear, the practice of conserving your resources to best advantage is a key to the successful and happy life. Answering the following yes-or-no questions should provide you with a clue to your present financial health:

1. Do you save something of every paycheck?
2. Do you make a budget?
3. Do you live within your budget?

4. Are you investing wisely by buying assets that protect you against inflation?
5. Do you search for bargains in small items, such as toothpaste and soap, as well as big ones like furniture and automobiles?
6. Do you weigh each purchase carefully rather than buy on impulse?

By the time you have completed The Templeton Plan and reviewed its twenty-one steps, you should be able to answer each of these questions with a confident yes.

STEP 13

PROGRESSING ONWARDS AND UPWARDS

JOHN TEMPLETON has been influenced in his life by Thomas Alva Edison, who said, "If you are doing something the same way you did it twenty years ago, then there must be a better way." To Templeton, this means that we should seek and welcome change. Change should be seen not as a problem but as a challenge—a form of progress that will lead to better methods for producing results.

Sometimes progress comes only after a careful assessment of your present position. "If things are not going well for you," said Roger Babson, founder of a business school, "begin your effort at correcting the situation by carefully examining the service you are rendering, and especially the spirit in which you are rendering it."

Follow-through is an all-important ingredient in making progress. To again quote William Feather: "Once you have sold a customer, make sure he is satisfied with your goods. Stay with him until the goods are used up or worn out. Your product may be of such long life that you will never sell him again, but he will sell you and your product to his friends."

And competition—the most difficult kind of all that pits you against your past performance—is at the heart of progress. "It is necessary," according to the seventeenth-century ruler Queen Christina of Sweden, "to try to surpass one's self always. This occupation ought to last as long as life."

Listed below are three other quotations on the secret of progress that have played a key role in John Templeton's thinking.

For artist John Carroll: "The whole story of human and personal progress is an unmitigated tale of denials today—denials of rest, denials of repose and comfort and ease and pleasure—that tomorrow may be richer."

C. R. Lawton, the industrialist, was convinced that "time is the one thing that can never be retrieved. One may lose and regain a friend; one may lose and regain money; opportunity once spurned may come again; but the hours that are lost in idleness can never be brought back to be used in gainful pursuits. Most careers are made or marred in the hours after supper."

And, finally, these words of clergyman Albert Johnson: "Unprogressiveness . . . is usually a function of wrong thinking rather than age. Inflexibility of mind and resistance to 'new ideas' crop up among the young as well as the old. To progress, one must be mentally alert and striving for self-improvement."

When John Templeton came to the conclusion that the field of management studies was in many ways unprogressive, he endowed Templeton College at Oxford, a graduate school in that discipline, named in memory of his mother and father. Templeton College teaches entrepreneurship, a sorely misunderstood and undertaught subject.

At the dedication ceremony for the new college, the British minister of education, Sir Keith Joseph, said that no English word existed meaning *entrepreneurship*. Templeton replied that the British equivalent might be *benefactor*, because entrepreneurs are essentially benefactors. They create jobs, pay taxes, and help the world to increase production. An entrepreneur tries to find ways to produce better-quality goods at lower prices. One of the secrets of progress is to train a nation of entrepreneurs.

Another way to progress onwards and upwards is to focus on the realm of the spirit. Through the Templeton Foundation Prizes for Progress in Religion, attention is concentrated on people who are doing new and original thinking in religion. Templeton regards progress in religion as more important to our success as people than progress in chemistry, medicine, or even peace.

He finds it encouraging that there are numerous new organizations working in the field of progress in religion, among them the American Scientific Affiliation, the Christian Medical Society, and the Research Scientists Christian Fellowship. If this tendency toward progress in religion continues, we may see a fulfillment of the prediction made sixty years ago by the electrical engineer Charles Steinmetz, who predicted that the greatest inventions of the twentieth century will be in the realm of the spirit, not the natural sciences.

But progress exists for all of us right now, today, in our own country, in ways that are not only spiritual. In a speech that John Templeton gave to the Financial Analysts Federation in 1984, he said, in part:

> What is the shape of the future? As long as freedom lives, the future is glorious.
>
> When I was born in Franklin County, Tennessee, the uniform wage for unskilled men was ten cents an hour. Now the average for factory workers is nine dollars. Even after adjusting for inflation, the increase is more than tenfold. The federal budget in nominal dollars is now almost 300 times as great as at the peak of prosperity in 1929. In my lifetime real consumption per person worldwide—that is, the standard of living in real goods—has more than quadrupled.
>
> A landmark for freedom was the publication 208 years ago of Adam Smith's great work called *An Inquiry into the Nature and Causes of the Wealth of Nations*. The necktie I wear today, bearing the likeness of Adam Smith, is supplied by the Philadelphia Society to commemorate that great liberation. In 208 years of relative freedom, the

yearly output of goods and services worldwide has increased more than a hundredfold. This is a hundredfold increase in real goods and services consumed, net after eliminating inflation.

Before Adam Smith, less than 1,000 corporations existed on earth, but now corporations are being created at the rate of 4,000 every business day. In the days of Adam Smith, 85 percent of the people were needed on the farm, but now less than 4 percent of the farms in America produce a surplus of food.

We now enjoy prosperity greater than ever dreamed of before this century. Will this level of progress continue in the future? If we are able to preserve and enhance freedom, these trends may continue and accelerate. We may expect more rapid change and wider fluctuations.

Life will be full of adventure and opportunity and never be dull or routine.

In America alone this year over $100 billion will be dedicated to research and development—more in one year in one nation than the total research for all the world's history before I was born. Awesome new blessings are visible also in health, entertainment, spiritual growth, and charity. In America alone over $50 billion will be donated to churches and charities this year. Each year the generous and voluntary giving by Americans alone exceeds the total income of all the world's people in any year before Adam Smith.

We should be overwhelmingly grateful to have been born in this century. The slow progress of prehistoric ages is over, and centuries of human enterprise are now miraculously bursting forth into flower. The evolution of human knowledge is accelerating, and we are reaping the fruits of generations of scientific thought: Only sixty years ago astronomers became convinced that the universe is 100 billion times larger than previously thought. More than half of the scientists who ever lived are alive today. More than half of the discoveries in the natural sciences have been made in this century. More than half of the goods produced since the earth was born have been produced in the two centuries since Adam Smith. Over half the books ever written were written in the last half-century. More new books are published each month than were written in the entire historical period before the birth of Columbus.

Discovery and invention have not stopped or even slowed down. Who can imagine what will be discovered if research continues to accelerate? Each discovery reveals new mysteries. The more we learn, the more we realize how ignorant we were in the past and how much more there is still to discover.

> If you do not fall down on your knees each day, with overwhelming gratitude for your blessings—your multiplying multitudes of blessings—then you just have not yet seen the big picture.

Now, of course, not all change is progress. Not all change leads to medical breakthroughs and scientific discoveries. Change can be either constructive or destructive. But the destructive forms tend to have a short life. The world is quick to eliminate those things that are not useful and progressive in the best sense of the word.

Those people who want to progress and be successful should focus on a goal that is productive and useful. They will be happy and fulfilled because their activities will help others.

The book *Future Shock* made the point that too much change is a problem, but actually there is never too much change. The book, if its theme had been stated properly, could have been called *Future Joy*, because change leads to progress, and progress to prosperity and happiness.

If you seek progress, always remain open-minded, read widely, travel extensively, continually ask questions, and be alert to new methods in your work. Most of all, seek. Those who do not seek are not likely to find. It says in Matthew 7:7–8: "Ask, and it will be given you; seek, and you will find; knock, and it will be opened unto you. For everyone who asks receives; and he who seeks finds; and to him who knocks it will be opened."

Consider progress in the field of medicine. Fifty percent

of all that is known has been discovered in the past twenty years. Ninety percent of all that is known has been discovered in the twentieth century.

We live in a world and a time of spiraling progress. We are better educated, better fed, and better housed than any people at any time in the history of the world. One of the greatest secrets of progress is to understand our good fortune—understand it and use it for worthwhile ends.

For John Templeton, the secret of progress is to continually test new methods, think of new ways to select investments, and test them rigorously to see which ones work. To stay ahead of other security analysts, he reads widely in professional journals and seeks to try new methods that are not yet popular with others.

Whatever field of work you have chosen as a career, it is vital that you study hard, that you try to become the most knowledgeable person in your field. It is important to examine your field in a world context, because your mind will grow more open and flexible if you understand what has happened under different circumstances in other cultures.

For example, John Templeton's son, a pediatric surgeon, as part of a delegation of American doctors visited Red China to study with Chinese doctors. They exchanged information on different methods and products, and the feeling was positive on both sides. The doctors from both countries felt they were learning something they did not already know—and a secret of progress is to constantly learn.

E. Parmalee Prentice, lawyer and author, made this

observation: "If anyone wants to understand the course of man on earth, he must consider the fact of the long pause, 3 million years on the level of savagery, 10,000 years on the level of dependence on the fruits of hard labor, and 150 years of sudden sharp rise. That is the time included in what we call progress in man's history."

Given this stunning rate of growth, think of all that we can accomplish, applying the plan discussed in this book, by the year 2000.

The secret of progress for all of us is to work hard in the present, always with an eye trained on the future.

In summary, Step 13 instructs the reader on principles that are necessary to move onwards and upwards. Practice them diligently and your rate of personal progress is bound to accelerate.

Among the main points covered:

1. The ability to handle change.
2. A willingness to pit yourself against your past performance.
3. Welcoming the entrepreneurial spirit within yourself.
4. Focusing on productive and useful goals.
5. Always striving to become the most knowledgeable person in your field.

STEP 14

CONTROLLING YOUR THOUGHTS FOR EFFECTIVE ACTION

THE WORDS *thought control* may well have an ominous ring to them, because we tend to associate thought control with controls imposed from the outside—for example, by repressive governments and certain religious cults. But John Templeton's approach is the exact opposite of these; it's inspirational. He practices and preaches imposing, from within, a discipline on one's thoughts and emotions. His theory of positive thought control is actually a deep form of self-control.

He says, "We're not products of circumstances or accident; we're products of what we think. Our thoughts influence our words, our deeds, what other people think of us, and whether or not they want to do business with us. If you hope to be productive and lead a happy life, you have to control your thoughts. The majority of people let their thoughts drift without making any attempt to control them. Thought control is hard work, but in the long run, with practice, it becomes easier and easier, like learning to play the piano. And when you've mastered the art of controlling your thoughts, you can make your mind a garden of indescribably beautiful flowers instead of a weed patch."

The Unity School of Christianity uses a phrase that sums up John Templeton's theory of positive thought control: "As you rule your mind, you rule the world." When Saint Paul recites the fruit of the spirit (Gal. 5:22), one of those nine virtues is self-control. It is John Templeton's strong conviction that people must pay attention to what is going on in their own minds. People are what they think. If you want to be a better person, you have to control what you're thinking.

Templeton's prodigious powers of concentration, perseverance, and hard work can be traced in large part to his development of personal techniques of thought control. This is a form of self-discipline that he believes is within reach of anyone, if that person will only resolve to develop this special personal power.

"Everyone has to work at it," he says. "And the harder you work, the easier it gets. A person will say to you, 'I just can't control my thoughts. They always wander away.' But that's because that person has not been trying. If you sit down at the piano and say, 'I can't play,' then you can't play because you've taken a negative mental attitude. But if you sit down with a positive approach, you'll find yourself making sudden strides forward. You're beginning to practice thought control."

Templeton acknowledges that there are some people, especially those involved in Eastern religions, who are quite successful at thought-restricting meditation. "But making your mind blank is extremely difficult—and what useful purpose is being served? To restate an old maxim, 'An idle mind really is the devil's workshop.'"

In contrast, the thought-control technique he advocates is what he calls the "crowding-out" method. He explains his approach this way: "If you fill your mind to capacity with thoughts that you think are good and productive, you won't have room for the bad ones. The ones you crowd out are feelings of envy, hatred, covetousness, self-centeredness, damaging criticism, revenge, and any time-wasting thoughts that are unproductive for your ultimate goals in life. Another method for crowding out negative thoughts is to quietly release them. You can even say to your thoughts, 'I lovingly release you to the vast nothingness from whence you came.'

As active and hardworking as Templeton is, he still makes time to practice the crowding out of extraneous matter. "It's directed thinking," he explains. "It shouldn't be thinking that is uncontrolled; the purpose is to clear and cleanse the mind."

Having learned to discipline his thinking, Templeton is able to focus a maximum amount of his energies on those matters he feels are of supreme importance: his investments and the learning and teaching of spiritual growth. Correct thought control has caused the direction of his entire life to become increasingly effective.

"Look at the result of controlled thinking in business," he says. "It's very difficult to build a corporation if you're incapable of directing your thoughts toward specific goals. You have to have an ordered mind to build any substantial organization, whether it's a business or a church or a charity."

Templeton also believes that correct thought control is a positive force. Listen to some of his observations on life: "If a stranger walks into the room, do you notice that he has a withered hand or do you notice the smile on his face? You can plant in your mind a wonderful concept and a good relationship with that stranger if you look for what's good in him, not for what worries you about him.

"You can find what you want to find in any situation. I'm a great believer in the old story about the stranger who came to the gates of a city and asked, 'What kind of people live here?'

"The gatekeeper replied, 'What kind of people live in the place you come from?'

"The stranger answered, 'Oh, they were knaves and fools and thugs.'

"The gatekeeper said, 'You will find the same kind of people here.'

"Another stranger came to the gate and asked the same question. The gatekeeper again asked, 'What kind of people live in the place you come from?'

"And the stranger answered, 'They are loving and generous.'

"The gatekeeper told him, 'You will find the same kind of people here.'

"That's what our lives are all about. And what effective

thought control and success are all about. If you're looking for the good in every person, you'll ask yourself, 'Where can I see Jesus shining through in this man's personality or that woman's life?' And you'll find him when you look for him. Jesus is always there awaiting our recognition.

"As soon as you wake up in the morning, direct your thoughts toward five things you're deeply grateful for. That will set the pattern for your day. You can't be prey to all the negative emotions if your heart is full of joy and gratitude."

John Templeton's entire personal and business life seems directed toward thoughts and actions that build up rather than tear down. He consciously attempts to realize in practical, everyday terms the words of Saint Paul to the Philippians (4:8): "Finally, brethren, whatever is true . . . whatever is pure, whatever is lovely, whatever is gracious, if there is any excellence, if there is anything worthy of praise, think about these things." As much as any other passages of scripture, these words have become the slogan of Templeton's private and professional life.

Although a Presbyterian and not a member of the Unity School of Christianity, Templeton has profited from literature published by the latter. For example, these words of Charles Fillmore, from his book *Prosperity*, go right to the heart of what gives us our special power as human beings. They speak to the bright side of our existence, the success side: "You can do everything with the thoughts of your mind. They are under your absolute control. You can direct them. You can coerce them. You can hush them or crush them. You can dissolve them and put others in their place. There is no other spot in the universe where man has mastery. The dominion that is yours by divine right is over your own thoughts. When man apprehends this and commences to exercise that dominion, he has begun to open the way to God, the only door to God—through mind and thought."

Templeton's favorite quotations on the importance and benefits of controlling your thoughts include the following:

According to author Ernest Holmes: "Life is a mirror and will reflect back to the thinker what he thinks into it."

George Matthew Adams, author and advertising executive, said: "Everyone knows that weeds eat out the life of a garden and of the productive fields. The gardener and farmer alike each has to keep the weeding process alive. It's like that in the building and developing of character. No one knows our own faults and tendencies better than we do ourselves, so that it is up to each one of us to keep the weeds out, and to keep all growth vigorous and fruitful."

To quote Grenville Kleiser once again: "Just as you are unconsciously influenced by outside advertisement, announcement, and appeal, so you can vitally influence your life from within by autosuggestion. The first thing each morning, and the last thing each night, suggest to yourself specific ideas that you wish to embody in your character and personality. Address such suggestions to yourself, silently or aloud, until they are deeply impressed upon your mind."

College president James Allen believed that "our life is what our thoughts make it. A man will find that as he alters his thoughts toward things and other people, things and other people will alter toward him."

Thomas Dreier, author and editor, visualized the art of thinking in these terms: "Before a painter puts a brush to his canvas he sees his picture mentally. It is the mental concept that he externalizes with the help of paint and canvas. If you think of yourself in terms of a painting, what do you see? How do you appear to yourself? Is the picture one you think worth painting? You are what you think you are. You create yourself in the image you hold in your mind. What you are advertises what you think."

Charles Darwin, the great naturalist, stated that "the highest possible stage in moral culture is when we recognize that we ought to control our thoughts."

And George Matthew Adams once more: "We can accomplish almost anything within our ability if we but think that we can. Every great achievement in this world was first carefully thought out. . . . Think—but to a purpose. Think constructively. Think as you read. Think as you listen. Think as you travel and your eyes reveal new situations. Think as you work daily at your desk, or in the field, or while strolling. Think to raise and improve your place in life. There can be no advancement or success without serious thought."

In the opinion of John Homer Miller, college president and author of many inspirational books: "Your life is determined not so much by what life brings to you as by the attitude you bring to life; not so much by what happens to you as by the way your mind looks at what happens. Circumstances and situations do color life but you have been given the mind to choose what the color shall be."

Finally, these thoughts by two famous Americans: Washington Irving: "Great minds have purposes, others have wishes." And Ralph Waldo Emerson: "Do not spill thy soul in running hither and yon, grieving over the mistakes and vices of others. The one person whom it is most necessary to reform is yourself."

The message is clear. If properly conceived and executed, thought control becomes positive thought control, which in turn results in effective action.

Controlling our thoughts, rather than being controlled by them, is a key element on the road to success and happiness.

What are the valuable lessons we have learned in Step 14?

1. Do not think of "thought control" as a repressive tool out of George Orwell's *1984*. Rather, think of it as a positive force that will leave your mind clearer, more directed, and more effective.
2. Remember that you are what you think. If you think well of yourself, others will think well of you. Your mind creates the environment in which you live and function.
3. Practice the "crowding-out" method by filling your mind with good and productive thoughts. Soon there will be no room left for the bad ones.
4. The moment you wake up in the morning set your thought pattern for the day. Think of five things for

which you are deeply grateful and keep them in your mind.

We learned in Step 10 that we can be master of time and not its slave. Now, in Step 14, it is clear that we can also be master of our thoughts, directing them along channels that will lead us to a happy and successful life.

STEP 15

LOVING AS THE ESSENTIAL INGREDIENT

"THE BIBLE SPEAKS often about the meaning of love," John Templeton says. "In the Sermon on the Mount, we are told to love our enemies. We are told to love those who hate us. We are told to turn the other cheek. Some people scoff at this advice and call it impractical. But, in fact, it's extremely practical. There is really no other way to lead a truly successful life.

"After all, it's not so hard to love those who love you. Even sinners are capable of that. And it's easy to give to those who give to us. The Bible doesn't applaud us for that. But if we can give and expect nothing in return, if we can learn to love our enemies, if we can be merciful even as our father is merciful, we will be true sons of the most high.

"'Judge not,' it says in Matthew (7:2), 'that you be not judged.' Condemn not and you will be forgiven. Give and it will be given to you. Good measure, pressed down, shaken together, running over, will be put into your lap. For the measure you give will be the measure you get back."

John Templeton also stresses that it is important to love ourselves. By being able to experience self-love, we can love others more completely. All successful people radiate self-love as well as love for others. Remember that Jesus said, "You shall love your neighbor as yourself" (Mark 12:31). But he did not say that you must love your neighbor and not yourself. In order to become a clear channel for the unlimited love of God to travel through you and spread to all his other children, you must first love yourself.

To succeed in your career, you must love yourself. You also must love yourself before you can give love to others.

One of the laws of life states that by expressing love, you attract love. John Templeton has written that "love given multiplies while love hoarded shrinks." God is the source of all love, and if we open ourselves to receive his love, then we are able to radiate it to other people every day.

Ninety-nine percent of the people you meet have good motives and mean well. You must be sufficiently imaginative and sympathetic to see through a crust of self-consciousness and fear to the inner person. There is goodness there waiting to be released.

Happiness and harmony will enter your life if you form the habit of always blessing and praying for your opponent. Try to visualize your opponent as a needy person, starved for affection and understanding.

To quote Ordway Tead, author of many books on management and education: "More and more clearly every day, out of biology, anthropology, sociology, history, economic analysis, psychological insight, plain human decency, and common sense, the necessary mandate of survival that we shall love all our neighbors as we do ourselves is being confirmed and reaffirmed."

The fifth winner of the Templeton Foundation Prize for Progress in Religion was Chiara Lubich, founder of the Focolare movement. When Chiara was a young teacher, she read in the Bible that Jesus commands us to love all others, including the unlovable, with his degree of passion. She realized that she had not yet met the test.

She then assembled a group of young people and they discussed how they could learn to love as Jesus loved. Their discussions were successful. Chiara and the others began to express a much deeper form of love. The movement she founded is called Focolare, from the Italian word meaning "fireplace," named that because her followers radiate love just as a fireplace radiates heat.

All of those connected with the Focolare movement live ordinary lives as employees of companies or members of secular societies and organizations. So, in that sense, they are so low-profile as to be nearly invisible to the casual observer. But to the people who are in contact with them every day, they are likely to be a breath of fresh air in a stuffy office, or an energizing influence in an otherwise drab environment.

The purpose of the Focolare movement is to promote the unity of all peoples and unity between generations. By the witness of their experience of living the gospel, and through songs, mime, and dance, they launch the message of the gospel with exceptional results. Working together with help from all over the world, the Focolarini built a town for the

Bangwa tribe in the Cameroon in the late 1970s, complete with a hospital, schools, an electric generator, and small industries.

The key thing about the most effective Focolare adherents is that they have caught part of Chiara Lubich's original fire, which began to burn at those spiritual "fireplaces" in the bomb shelters of Trent, Italy, during the Second World War, when Chiara was a young woman. They have learned how to love—how to love all people, black and white, rich and poor—how to love with Jesus' passion.

The main lesson from Chiara and her Focolare movement is essentially the same as Jesus' double-edged message in the Sermon on the Mount: It is important not to practice your piety before others and, in effect, sound a fanfare each time you go to worship or perform a good deed. But, at the same time, it's essential not to hide the light of your faith under a bushel so that no one knows the direction from whence it came.

In the mountains of Tennessee, there is an old ditty—a longtime favorite of John Templeton's—that goes, "You never can tell the depth of the well by the length of the handle of the pump." If we judge by appearances, by how people dress, or how they speak or look, we are making a mistake. Deal with the inner person. Approach others with kindness and patience and you will be repaid with a glimpse of their common humanity.

In all facets of life, whether in business or in family or social life, the successful people are the ones who reach out.

They give of themselves. They know that they are no better than others and that others are not their enemies.

To illustrate the basic truth in the teaching of the "Golden Rule" as given by Jesus in the Sermon on the Mount, here is the same idea as expressed in other cultures and religions. We can learn from these examples how to make love the essential ingredient in our lives.

Zoroastrianism: "Do as you would be done by."

Confucianism: "Do not unto others what you would not they should do unto you."

Buddhism: "One should seek for others the happiness one desires for oneself. Hurt not others with that which pains yourself."

Hinduism: "Guard and do by the things of others as they would do by their own. This is the sum of duty; do naught to others which if done by thee would cause thee pain."

Egyptian: "He sought for others the good he desired for himself. Let him pass on."

Chinese: "What you would not wish done to yourself, do not to others."

Persian: "Do as you would be done by."

Taoism: "Regard your neighbor's gain as your own gain, and your neighbor's loss as your own."

Judaism: "What is hurtful to yourself, do not to your fellow man."

Islam: "Let none of you treat his brother in a way he would

himself dislike to be treated. No one of you is a believer until he loves for his brother what he loves for himself."

In summary, Step 15 teaches us:

1. That it is easy to love our friends. The hard job is to love our enemies, and yet that is the goal we must pursue if we are to make loving the essential ingredient in our lives.
2. That we must allow ourselves to love ourselves. All love for others radiates outward from within.
3. That we must practice kindness and patience with others to begin to glimpse our common humanity.
4. That it is the successful and happy person who is willing to risk reaching out to others.

STEP 16

MAXIMIZING THE POWER OF YOUR FAITH

In the book *The Natural Way* by Lao-Tzu, a Chinese philosopher born six centuries before Jesus, are lines that reveal as eloquently as any from Western thought a method for moving toward the light within ourselves: "Moved by deep love, a man is courageous. And with frugality, a man becomes generous, and he who does not desire to be ahead of the world becomes the leader of the world."

By studying the behavior of those with whom we come in contact, it should soon be apparent that the most happy and productive among them are the ones who rejoice in the good fortune of others. And it is not a counterfeit form of rejoicing. They truly care.

During his years as an investment counselor for hundreds of families, Templeton has noticed that successful people consistently care about others. They seek to find good in them. They are quick to sense the best qualities that dwell within others.

Successful people never fail to mention the positive traits of other people. They point out good qualities and treat the more negative ones as though they didn't exist. They proceed on the theory that by playing to someone's strengths and overlooking the weaknesses, those weaknesses will not have fertile soil in which to grow. This is a way of putting the power of your faith into action—the power that spells success.

You should be particularly charitable to those with whom you are in competition. Multitudes of friends will be drawn to you if you're careful never to say anything negative about a competitor. When John Templeton was in his formative stages as a young businessman, he learned one of the laws of life: "If you can't say something good, keep your mouth shut."

Successful and happy people will try to express their empathy in all circumstances. This means putting yourself inside the minds and hearts of others and feeling the effect your words and attitudes will have on them. This insight will help you to speak only those words that offer affirmation and a positive result. It is wise to pray, "Oh Lord, give me the courage to improve what I can improve, the patience to endure what I cannot improve, and the wisdom to tell the difference between the two."

Empathy is a quality that can be practiced and perfected. In moments of quiet meditation it will be helpful to repeat to yourself the words of Christ: "You shall love the Lord your God with all your heart, and with all your soul, and with all your mind, and with all your strength. . . . You shall love your neighbor as yourself" (Mark 12:30–31).

It is important to meditate on how circumscribed is our knowledge and how infinite is the knowledge of God. God's creations are thousands of times more numerous and mysterious than the things we, his children, have yet observed or understood.

Realizing our human limitations in perceiving the full extent of God's universe is what John Templeton calls the humble approach. Ninety-nine and nine-tenths of all that humans comprehend has been learned in the last one-millionth of the earth's history, 50 percent in the latest 1 percent of that one-millionth. Imagine, then, how much there is that we do not know, which remains hidden from us!

When meditating on the laws of life in high school, John Templeton made a lifelong resolution: "Never write down what you don't want published. Whatever you say or write should be intended to uplift and inspire the reader and should never be harmful." Even at an early age he understood the importance of faith for a happy and successful life.

To fully maximize the power of our faith, we must expunge all envy from our hearts. If friends win the lottery, we should rejoice with them as though we had won it ourselves. It costs nothing and makes their joy in having won even greater. We should never, under any circumstances, begrudge others their good fortune. John Templeton often recounts the parable of the workers in the vineyard from Matthew (20:1–16) because, to him, it is a clear and beautiful lesson on the sin of envy and the virtue of Christian equity.

"In the kingdom of heaven," he says, "there was once a

landowner who went out early one morning to hire workers for his vineyard. He offered them a day's wages and sent them off to work. Three hours later, when he checked on their progress, he saw some men standing around with nothing to do. 'If you want to work for me,' he said, 'I'll pay you a fair wage.' They agreed.

"In the early afternoon he went out again, found more idle men, and made the same arrangement with them. An hour before sunset he found still another group standing there.

"He said to them, 'Why are you standing around like this all day with nothing to do?'

"And they answered, 'No one's hired us.'

"So he told them, 'Well, you can work for me.'

"When evening fell, the owner of the vineyard said to his steward, 'Give the workers their pay, beginning with those who came last and ending with the first.'

"Those who had started work an hour before sunset came forward and were paid the full day's wage, as were all the others. But the men who had come first and worked the longest expected something extra. When they were paid the same amount as the others, they got angry at their employer. They said, 'Those fellows didn't do nearly as much work as us and yet you gave them equal pay. That's not fair. We sweated all day long in the blazing sun.'

"The owner said to them, 'I am not being unfair to you. You agreed on the wage for the day, didn't you? So be satisfied. You got what you bargained for. I decided to pay the last man the same as you. Surely I am free to do what I like with my own money. Why be jealous because I'm kind?'

"The moral of this tale? Be a good worker in the vineyard and never begrudge anyone his good fortune. If, for example, you have a customer who has had great success, feel truly happy for him and express your happiness in his accomplishment. If you have a supplier or an employee who has received an honor, feel just as proud and happy as if you had received the honor."

The power of faith in action—across conference tables or lunch tables—is a revolution, a new way of thinking, feeling, and acting. It needs to be acquired and is worth every single moment of the effort involved.

In summation, John Templeton has this thought: "What you give out comes back to you. If you are genuinely excited and joyful about someone else's good fortune, you will have made a friend for life. People will admire you for your generous expanse of spirit. And in the end, admiration, success, and honor will come to the person who is truly joyful over the good fortune of others."

In Step 16 we learn that the power of faith is a crucial ingredient in the formula for success and happiness. Answer the following questions and score yourself on your current level of faith.

1. Do you rejoice in the good fortune of others?
2. Do you remain silent if you can't find something good to say about someone?

3. Are you quick to express empathy?
4. Are you careful about expressing criticism?
5. Do you make an effort to expunge all envy from your heart?
6. Do you work at being a humble person?

If you can answer yes to these questions, your faith is strong and your prospects for happiness and success are excellent.

STEP 17

RECEIVING STRENGTH THROUGH PRAYER

WHEN ASKED the secret of his success, John Templeton gives prayer the top priority. Giving thanks to God, he feels, provides believers with a strength that can raise them to new heights of performance and insight.

Templeton's approach to prayer relates to his concept of God and God's creative process. God is infinite. Everything that exists in the universe and beyond the universe is God. That means that the visible universe is only a small particle of God and is itself a manifestation of God. By the word *manifest*, Templeton means that which a human being can know. Thus one little particle of God has become known to us through gravity, light waves, pulsars, and other things that enable us to perceive a few features of the universe.

Templeton believes that we ourselves are one of God's more recent creations, and, again, we represent only the tiniest fraction of God. If we realize this truth and try to bring ourselves into oneness with God, if we become humble tools in his hands and clear channels for his purposes, we will be able to accomplish much more than if we fail to realize that oneness. And what we do accomplish will be more likely to endure.

No matter what you do in life—enrolling in college, getting married, buying a stock, doing a tax return, extracting a tooth—you will do it better if you start with prayer. And the prayer should be that God will use you as a conduit for his love and wisdom. Your prayer should say that the words you speak and the actions you take will be in harmony with God's purposes, for the benefit of his children, and never meant only for selfish goals.

If this is your prayer, everything that follows is bound to be more successful and your life will radiate joy. With a mind no longer in conflict, you are far less likely to disagree with your associates or do something you'll regret later, on cool reflection. So your decision making will be improved if you try to bring yourself into contact with God and into a oneness with his purposes. By making a profound effort to be one with God and God's children through prayer, everything you do in life will turn out far better, including your business decisions. Success will seek you out.

Templeton's personal technique for getting into harmony with God—whether he is concerned with his children or his business or his many charities—is to pray simply, "Thy will be done." This approach helps him to empty his mind of all preconceptions so that he can give himself over more completely to what he perceives as God's guidance.

He prays often during the day. And if there is an especially complex problem to solve, or decision to make, he'll try to wait a day and spend extra time in prayer before he acts.

Before going to sleep that night, he says, "God, I have done the best I can. Now guide me in this decision." Very often, the next morning he has a solution that is better than anything he had considered the day before. Putting yourself in God's hands through prayer and then working as hard and honestly as you can is the mark of a successful person.

Templeton also encourages his associates to participate in prayer, even when they are somewhat reluctant to get involved. In public meetings, he has found that it is more effective to give people very little advance warning; sometimes, an hour before a meeting is to start, he'll say casually to an associate, "I'm going to ask you to open with prayer." That gives the person a little time to prepare, though not so much that he becomes overly nervous or self-conscious.

Templeton feels that it is a good policy to rotate prayer at regular meetings among a number of people, because then the practice is less likely to harden into a ritual. The person praying benefits, and those listening benefit as their friends pray. The ceremony takes on a family, intimate quality, and Templeton's principle of success through prayer is spread among many.

A marked emphasis on prayer was not a part of Templeton's early investment years. His career as an investment counselor can be divided into two equal parts. For the first twenty years ("when I was a worse backslider than at any other time in my life," he says), there was no prayer at investment meetings. But, for the past twenty years, all meetings have opened and closed with prayer. And it's a fact that his stress on prayer has coincided with the most successful performance period of the Templeton Growth Fund.

Skeptics may downgrade the importance of prayer in Templeton's investment selections. They may say that he was successful even before he began to pray regularly or inject prayer so openly into his business sessions. And they may further argue that he would have reached the same high level of success as an investor even if he had neglected prayer altogether.

Templeton disagrees. Prayer has given him, he's convinced, a clarity of mind and depth of insight that have been key factors in his success. Through the power of prayer, he sees much more deeply into himself and into others. He is certain that without prayer he would never have become the outstanding success that he is.

He says: "Everyone who hopes to be a successful person should start each day with prayer. Like Solomon, do not offer self-centered prayers, but pray for wisdom and understanding. Try to end each prayer with the words, 'Thy will be done, O Lord, not mine.' The Lord's purposes are much wiser than our purposes.

"Pray that you are overwhelmingly grateful for your blessings. If you are healthy, thank the Lord for that. If your children are happy, thank him for that. Thank him for the things you have instead of asking for what you don't have.

"Begin each day by thinking of five blessings, or ten blessings. If you make a practice of doing that, your whole day will go more usefully and constructively.

"You will be far along the road to success."

One of Templeton's favorite prayers is from Romans (12:9–18). He feels that there exists nowhere in the Bible a better prescription for success and happiness: "Let love be genuine; hate what is evil, hold fast to what is good; love one another with brotherly affection; outdo one another in showing honor. Never flag in zeal, be aglow with the Spirit, serve the Lord. Rejoice in your hope, be patient in tribulation, be constant in prayer. Contribute to the needs of the saints, practice hospitality.

"Bless those who persecute you; bless and do not curse them. Rejoice with those who rejoice, weep with those who weep. Live in harmony with one another; do not be haughty, but associate with the lowly; never be conceited. Repay no one evil for evil, but take thought for what is noble in the sight of all. If possible, so far as it depends upon you, live peaceably with all."

Step 17 teaches us that God is infinite and that just as the visible universe is only a small particle of God, we are only an infinitesimal part of the visible universe. No matter what we accomplish, we have done it under God. If we are humble, if we can bring ourselves to realize that we are one of God's more recent creations, perhaps not even his most important one, we stand a better chance to be balanced people who will lead happy and successful lives.

Try these exercises to enhance the strength of your prayer:

1. Pray frequently.
2. Pray that God will use you as a channel for his love and wisdom.
3. Pray that you will be in harmony with God's purposes.
4. Pray that what you say and do will be for the benefit of everyone.
5. Put yourself in God's hands.
6. Be overwhelmingly grateful for all your blessings.
7. Pray simply, "Thy will be done."

STEP 18

GIVING AS A WAY OF LIFE

WHEN HE WAS in his late thirties, John Templeton began the practice of tithing (and sometimes double-tithing), giving to churches and charities 10 percent or more of his earnings. That was about the time his mother and first wife died, a time when he began to be increasingly in touch with his religious sensibilities.

In later years, he contributed to various religious and educational causes, including the Templeton Prize. After his death, the Templeton Foundation and Templeton Religious Trust will have more than enough capital to carry on this program permanently.

There are many interpretations of the meaning of this kind of generous giving. Some might refer to the biblical principle that "the more you give, the more you'll receive." The particular references that support this idea would include the following:

> He who sows sparingly will also reap sparingly, and he who sows bountifully will also reap bountifully . . . for God loves a cheerful giver. (2 Cor. 9:6–7)

> Give, and it will be given to you; good measure, pressed down, shaken together, running over, will be put into your lap. For the measure you give will be the measure you get back. (Luke 6:38)

> Bring the full tithes into the storehouse, that there may be food in my house; and thereby put me to the test, says the Lord of hosts, if I will not open the windows of heaven for you and pour down for you an overflowing blessing. (Mal. 3:10)

Just as skeptics have downgraded the power of prayer as a key component in Templeton's rise to success, there are those who see no relation between his success and his increasing giving. But giving, for Templeton, grows naturally from prayer. Material success, he feels, is much more likely to come to those willing to give some of their wealth away. He honors the letter and spirit of the biblical passages just quoted and is ready to attribute his success to the strength of those principles in his life. He believes literally in the Hindu proverb that says, "They who give have all things; they who withhold have nothing."

Templeton invests his money not only in companies that will produce high-interest income but also in possible research projects in religion that resemble current research in the physical world of science. The term *religious research* might seem ambiguous, but John Templeton would define it as religion borrowing the tools of scientific investigation in order to understand itself. To serve as illustrations, here are a few of the various possibilities for research in religion:

- ▹ The ministerial longevity phenomenon: Records kept for 200 years by the Presbyterian Ministers' Fund, one of the oldest life insurance companies in the world, show that Christian ministers live ten years longer than other men. Why? A research team of ministers, theologians, psychologists, and physicians might discover interesting information on this phenomenon.
- ▹ Healing as miracle: Several church denominations have collected thousands of well-documented cases of divine healing, but they have not yet been subjected to scientific studies by critically minded doctors, historians, and sociologists. Such studies might reveal how, why, when, and to whom divine healing occurs.
- ▹ The rise-up-and-walk problem: Some doctors agree that patients' rate of healing, after having the same operation, varies as greatly as 300 percent among different people. In addition to studying the biological, anatomical, chemical, and psychological reasons for this, studies into the religious attitudes of patients might show a correlation between spiritual conviction and physical recovery.
- ▹ The joy-to-the-world question: Recent research has been conducted by psychologists on this question

of why some people experience unexpected, intense rushes of joy while others do not. A theological consultant to these studies might be able to discover what spiritual factors contribute to the experience of joy. Are people who trust wholeheartedly in God generally more joyous than a control group of agnostics? Which groups of people describe themselves as happy most of the time? Which do not?

- ▹ Psychiatric health: Do people who become charismatic Christians through the experience of Pentecost need psychiatric help less than they did before? Maybe scientists could collect statistics on the frequency of visits to psychiatrists before and after the charismatic experience.
- ▹ God and the psychotic: Psychiatric teams that include pastoral theologians might embark on new studies of patients in mental institutions to correlate types of insanity or psychoses with previous religious convictions. Are there significantly larger or smaller percentages of mental patients who were healing practitioners, doctors, clergy, or scientists?
- ▹ The prodigal-sons-and-daughters problem: Do youthful offenders come from families in which religious worship is strong, average, or weak? Ministers and theologians should participate in these kinds of studies. It should be possible to collect statistics on young persons indicted for crimes to discover what

> proportion attended Sunday schools or were reared by parents who regularly attended church or synagogue or mosque.

These are only a few examples of possible research projects in religion that institutes, academies, and seminaries might undertake.

By investing in projects such as these, Templeton magnifies the joy and sense of meaning he receives from earning profits on his investments. That sense of joy and accomplishment causes him to work even harder and more creatively to make more money so that a large share of that money can go for worthy causes.

The positive feeds on the positive. Giving leads to greater giving and becomes a way of life. Templeton gives and gains, and gives and gains even more. It is a cycle that continually feeds on itself in a positive way. And throughout this process, Templeton's own sense of gratitude and spiritual accomplishment has grown as well.

Thanksgiving inspires giving, not only in the person who is thankful but in the one who hears the thanksgiving. To Templeton, Thanksgiving is an important and neglected holiday, celebrated by only six of the world's nations, among them the United States, Canada, and Brazil. For more than twenty-five years Templeton and his wife have mailed to their friends pictures of their family with inspirational messages of thanksgiving.

Templeton has written: "Thanksgiving opens the door to spiritual progress." Those who are full of thanksgiving are givers, and the successful are grateful givers.

He says: "Each of us should cultivate a feeling of gratitude. Try to find opportunities each day to compliment the people you work with. To thank them for their contributions. Because they will do more, knowing they are appreciated.

"Be grateful that the world is 90 percent blessings and only 10 percent problems and struggles. As the eminent physician and writer Lewis Thomas has said, there is mostly healthiness and very little sickness in our bodies, and we should never forget that. Existence is more good than bad, more honest than crooked, more contentment than sorrow.

"We have everything to be grateful for, and when we're grateful, we give."

Giving, Templeton is convinced, is a method where a person can grow and become truly a success.

Feeling as he does about Thanksgiving, John Templeton praises his friend Peter Stewart, who organized Thanksgiving Square, a beautiful triangle of land in the heart of downtown Dallas. A tower has been erected on this land in the form of an upward spiral, and inside this spiral are illustrations and quotations from Thanksgivings since America's first celebration of the holiday. People from the offices around Thanksgiving Square go there and pray during the business day.

In a sense, John Templeton sees giving as a test of maturity. Those who are truly grown up give. The immature do not. It is wise, he feels, to practice giving in every area of life. Give thoughtful, well-reasoned advice. Give thanks. Give attention. Give prizes and honors. If you are lonely, give. If you are bored, give. Take on charity jobs. Help with fundraising.

There is no greater gift you can give than to help another person become a giver. As a child, Templeton was taught always to give the larger piece of cake to the other person. At meetings, he believes in taking a backseat unless asked to come forward. The Bible teaches us that if anyone would be first among us, let him first become the servant of all.

As evidence of spiritual progress, Americans are giving over $70 billion yearly to churches and charity. That is ten times as much charity as was given in the entire world in any year before this century.

John Templeton and his wife Irene learned the meaning of the words "You can never outgive the Lord" when they founded the Templeton Prize in 1973. The prize program put them in touch with the wonderful new methods and thinking being done in every religion. They sought out and studied the great adventures at work in the world's religious community, and they therefore derived more benefit from the program than anyone.

It has been well said that "we give thee but thine own, whate'er our gifts may be. For all that we have, dear Lord, is but a trust from thee."

Below are listed John Templeton's favorite quotations on being a giver. They are sure steps along the road to success.

Edwin Arlington Robinson, the American poet, wrote these lines: "There are two kinds of gratitude: The sudden kind we feel for what we take; the larger kind we feel for what we give."

Industrialist R. A. Hayward believed that "for every action there is an equal and opposite reaction. If you want to receive a great deal, you first have to give a great deal. If each individual will give of himself to whomever he can, wherever he can, in any way that he can, in the long run he will be compensated in the exact proportion that he gives."

According to Henry Emerson Fosdick, religious leader and author of many best-selling books: "One of the most amazing things ever said on this earth is Jesus' statement: 'He that is greatest among you shall be your servant.' Nobody has one chance in a billion of being thought really great after a century has passed except those who have been the servant of all. That strange realist from Bethlehem knew that."

Author Albert Pine believed that "what we have done for ourselves alone dies with us. What we have done for others and the world remains and is immortal."

Clergyman and college president Paul D. Moody said: "The measure of a man is not the number of his servants but in the number of people whom he serves."

Andrew Cordier, then dean of the Columbia University School of International Affairs, feels that "it should be our purpose in life to see that each of us makes such a contribution as will enable us to say that we, individually and collectively, are a part of the answer to the world problem and not part of the problem itself."

Calvin Coolidge offered this aphorism on the subject of giving: "No person was ever honored for what he received. Honor has been the reward for what he gave."

And the words of the mythical Paul Bunyan: "A man there was, and they called him mad; the more he gave, the more he had."

Last, according to clergyman and author J. Richard Sneed: "When we act upon the formula of 'giving service,' we seem to get what we want and we also get it from the other person. In the high art of serving others, workers sustain their morale, management keeps its customers, and the nation prospers. One of the indisputable lessons of life is that we cannot get or keep anything for ourselves alone unless we also get it for others."

John Templeton's advice to those seeking the road to success is to give—to give wholeheartedly. To the giver all things will be returned.

After completing Step 18, ask yourself these questions:

1. Do I give money each year to charities?
2. Do I tithe to a church?
3. Do I believe that life without giving is a hollow existence?
4. Is it my philosophy that what I am given—in terms of my abilities, my intelligence, and my material

success—should be returned to the world in some form that will help others?

By answering yes to these questions, you are already a giver and your life is enriched. Keep in mind that spiritual progress and material success are closely connected. Never be afraid to give. Serve others and you serve yourself.

STEP 19

WINNING THROUGH HUMILITY

IN ORDER TO experience the emotions of humility and awe, emotions indispensable to the success-bound person, John Templeton often reflects on these words of Albert Einstein: "The most wonderful thing we can experience is the mysterious. It is the source of all art and science. He to whom this emotion is a stranger, who can no longer pause to wonder and stand rapt in awe, is as good as dead; his eyes are closed."

Templeton wrote in his study of religion and science, *The Humble Approach*:

> We are perched on the frontiers of future knowledge. Even though we stand upon the enormous mountain of information collected over the last five centuries of scientific progress, we have only fleeting glimpses of the future. To a large extent, the future lies before us like a vast wilderness of unexplored reality. The God who created and sustains his evolving universe through eons of progress and development has not placed our

> generation at the tag end of the creative process. He has placed us at a new beginning. We are here for the future.
>
> Our role is crucial. As human beings we are endowed with mind and spirit. We can think, imagine, and dream. We can search for future trends through the rich diversity of human thought. God permits us in some ways to be co-creators with him in his continuing act of creation.
>
> Scientists have steadily been changing their concepts of the universe and laws of nature, but the progression is always away from smaller self-centered or man-centered concepts. Evidence is always accumulating that things seen are only one aspect of the vastly greater unseen realities. Man's observational abilities are very limited, and so are his mental abilities. Should we not focus our lives on the unseen realities and not on the fleeting appearances? Should we not kneel down in humility and worship the awesome, infinite, omniscient, eternal Creator?

In *The Humble Approach*, Templeton has called for research efforts to study and enhance spiritual progress. He feels that such efforts should be pursued with the same level of urgency that goes into research in scientific fields.

But how do spiritual progress and a perception of God's

invisible universe help people in their lives and in their work? John Templeton answers by placing his hands, palms down, on a table. "Up until this century," he says, "people would have said that this table is reality. But now natural scientists know that it is in fact 99 percent nothingness. What appears as reality to your eyes is just a configuration, a constantly changing vibration. What we conceive of as reality is really appearance.

"The only reality is the Creator. He and his works are the only permanent things. I would put it this way: The things that are unseen are reality. The illusions, the temporary things, are what we see."

To be successful, each of us must build his own soul in imitation of the Creator. That means we must appreciate other people. We must always try to express our faith in all situations—at work, at home, with friends. Our spirit must be humble.

The unseen—the beauty that exists as potential in all of us—is what makes us alive. If we don't believe we're alive, we will never find success. But if we are alive, we will understand that the only true reality is God; when we have reached that stage of maturity and moral development, we will be constantly productive and useful. We will become more outgoing. We will feel a surge of joy over the good fortune of others. The desire to do something of lasting benefit will be constantly at the forefront of our thoughts. We will be that much closer to being successful and happy people.

To quote again from *The Humble Approach*:

> By learning humility, we find that the purpose of life on earth is vastly deeper than any human mind can grasp. Diligently, each child of God should seek to find and obey God's purpose, but none be so egotistical as to think that he or she comprehends the infinite mind of God.
>
> Every person's concept of God is too small. Through humility we can begin to get into true perspective the infinity of God. This is the humble approach. Are we ready to begin the formulation of a humble theology which can never become obsolete? This would be a theology really centered upon God and not upon our own little selves.

But what are the practical applications of a sense of humility and an appreciation of God's infinite powers? John Templeton believes there are many, not least of which is patience—patience in all things. The depth of his belief has given him a singular—and singularly successful—perspective on how to run a mutual funds business.

He believes that if you apply the same methods of selection that other people are applying, you'll get the same things they're buying and you'll have the same results. But Templeton tries to have the long-range viewpoint—the one that comes from a deep well of patience and self-belief. He will buy those things that others have not yet thought about. Then he waits until the short-term prospects become good and other people start coming in and buying the stock, thus pushing the price up.

It is also important to note here that Templeton does not simply delegate research tasks to those who work for him and leave it at that. He could. He works as hard as anyone, and he's much more successful than all but a few; it is accurate to say that his success has put him in a position to exercise his considerable powers to their fullest in any way that he might see fit. He has a task force of associates, officers, and other employees in his companies who contribute their talents to the formulation of portfolios. But he does a prodigious amount of personal research so that he can make an informed decision about what to do when a stock comes up for his consideration.

John Templeton knows that his love of work, of his family, of his colleagues, and of life itself stems directly from his love of God. One of his favorite biblical quotations is 1 John 4:7–12:

> Beloved, let us love one another; for love is of God, and he who loves is born of God and knows God. He who does not love does not know God; for God is love. In this the love of God was made manifest among us, that God sent his only son into the world, so that we might live through him. In this is love, not that we loved God but that he loved us and sent his Son to be the expiation for our sins. Beloved, if God so loved us, we also

> ought to love one another. No man has ever seen God; if we love one another, God abides in us and his love is perfected in us.

If you remain humble and steadfast in your love of God and man, you will have taken one of the most important steps on the road to success. Your humility will make you a winner.

Step 18 taught us the meaning of humility through giving. Now in Step 19, we extend our search for humility by examining our relationship to God's invisible universe.

Before proceeding to Step 20, begin to practice the following mental exercises:

1. Try to appreciate some positive quality in all the people you meet.
2. Try to be humble in all your actions.
3. Try to face even the most difficult situations with equanimity and patience.
4. Learn to feel joy over the good fortune of others.
5. Never forget that the only reality is the Creator; he and his works are the only permanent things on this earth.

Through the exercise of will, we can come closer each day to becoming truly successful and happy people.

STEP 20

DISCOVERING NEW FRONTIERS

AMONG THE NUMEROUS dictionary definitions of *frontier*, there are two that most clearly explain John Templeton's feelings about carefully calculated risks and challenge in the face of adversity: "The farthermost limits of knowledge or achievement with respect to a particular subject" and "a new field that offers scope for exploitative or developmental activity."

From an early age, young John showed a willingness to say yes to experience. Although he was the first in his rural county to take college entrance examinations, he attended Yale. After he graduated from college, he went off to England on a Rhodes scholarship. You would think that such a radical change might have thrown a boy from a small Tennessee town, but, in fact, the opposite was true: He thrived on the challenge.

He took advantage of a program called Ryderising, a system of travel set up by Lady Frances Ryder to expose American students to proper British families. Many students were too shy or socially backward to join the program, but John immediately jumped at it. Soon he met many interesting and distinguished families.

His willingness to try new experiences taught him much about the world and helped him on his way to success. It's important to understand that, for reasons John sensed subconsciously, the personal contacts he was making and the experiences he was having would later prove invaluable to him. So he overcame whatever timidity he might have felt and threw himself enthusiastically into a variety of strange experiences and personal encounters.

He was not afraid of new frontiers; he welcomed them. Whether it was the frontier of Yale, or traveling to England on his Rhodes scholarship, or touring far-flung and exotic places in the world on a few hundred dollars, or making the decision to enter a field—mutual fund investing—almost before such a field existed, John Templeton was convinced that there were new frontiers to discover.

Success-bound people have to believe in themselves, because the frontier exists inside of them. Jesus' teaching concerning this is found in Luke (17:21) where we are reminded that "the kingdom of God is not coming with signs to be observed; . . . for behold, the kingdom of God is in the midst of you." This is the true frontier that we must explore: our own inner being, our own divinity. Forgetting our divinity or turning away from it creates a sense of separation from God. As we learn to remember our oneness with God, we will automatically realize every person's oneness with God and with us.

Templeton puts great store in the words of Charles E. Kettering, a scientist whose research included the invention of automotive starting and ignition systems: "There will always be a frontier where there is an open mind and a willing hand."

And those of the English novelist Tobias Smollett: "Who bravely dares must sometimes risk a fall."

And these of Antoine de Saint Exupéry, the French pilot and author: "A rock pile ceases to be a rock pile the moment a single man contemplates it, bearing within him the image of a cathedral."

And especially the words of President Theodore Roosevelt:

> It is impossible to win the great prizes of life without running risks, and the greatest of all prizes are those connected with the home. No father and mother can hope to escape sorrow and anxiety, and there are dreadful moments when death comes very near to those we love, even if for the time being it passes by. But life is a great adventure, and the worst of all fears is the fear of living. There are many forms of success, many forms of triumph. But there is no other success that in any shape or way approaches that which is open to most of the many men and women who have the right ideals. These are the men and women who see that it is the intimate and homely things

> that count most. They are the men and women who have the courage to strive for the happiness that comes only with labor and effort and self-sacrifice, and those whose joy in life springs in part from power of work and sense of duty.

When young Templeton returned to the United States after completing his Rhodes scholarship and journeying through India, China, Japan, and much of the Middle East, he was a wiser young man for all of the challenges and risks he had eagerly accepted. He had learned something about the lifestyles and attitudes of a variety of people.

He was ready to settle down to the challenge of work. When two solid job offers in New York came through, he took the lower-paying job. Again, he was ready to gamble, to move out to the frontier. He felt that the position with Fenner & Beane, a stock brokerage firm that just three months earlier had established its investment counseling division, would give him an opportunity to learn much and to learn it quickly.

Two years later, having taken certain factors into consideration that reduced the risk of his sizable investment, he made his now-famous offer to buy $100 worth of every stock on the stock exchanges that was selling for no more than a dollar per share. As preparation, he had done thorough research during the previous two years on the performance of stocks selling for less than one dollar, and in case his theory should prove wrong, he had sufficient assets to cover the $10,000 he borrowed.

As you can see, people on the road to success are not afraid to take calculated risks. They prepare carefully for their forays into uncharted territory.

The ability to take risks and accept challenges is keenest among those with deep religious faith. Faith means "having respect for" or "standing in awe of," which is the opposite of the blindness that skeptics often associate with faith.

Basically faith, like hope, involves trust. In what or whom do we trust? We learn to trust the eternal, not the transient. Understand the transient and use it for your own ends, but do not place lasting hope in it.

It is said that faith can move mountains. Faith gives courage; it enables people to seek out new territory, stretch their abilities, gamble for the greater good, and, in times of trouble, they will know how to deal with adversity.

In February 1951 tragedy entered John Templeton's life. His first wife was killed in a highway accident while they were touring Bermuda on motorbikes.

"I had three small children," Templeton recalls. "I didn't know how to be a mother to them, but I had to try. I couldn't spend all day with them because I was in the midst of trying to build a business and earn a living."

This tragedy was magnified for Templeton because his mother had died a few months before, in September 1950. Within the space of six months he had lost the two most important women in his life. He was thrown back as never before upon his own spiritual resources.

He remarried in 1958, to Irene Reynolds Butler. She supported him fully in his religious pursuits as his spiritual sensitivities began to sharpen. He had met the challenge of the death of two loved ones—there can be no greater challenge—by developing a deeper belief in God. Death, too, was a frontier that had to be charted, mapped out, and lived in.

Then, as the 1960s unfolded, Templeton's spiritual and professional lives came together in a way that was to make him one of the most successful investors in this century. First of all, the group of mutual funds that he had established was doing well. An insurance company offered to buy him and the seven other shareholders out. He had been having increasingly strong feelings that it was time for him to devote more effort and financial support to spiritual matters, and this opportunity seemed an advantageous way to reduce his work load and focus his energies on religion.

As he put it, "I had spent my early career helping people with their personal finances, but helping them to grow spiritually began to seem so much more important."

The Templetons selected the Bahamas as their permanent home base—a place where they could live among people of deep spirituality in a setting of natural beauty, a place conducive to religious study and work. And he began to devote another thirty hours a week to religious and philanthropic work.

Through good times and bad, success-bound people will

seek out new frontiers to explore, to settle, to enhance. They will gladly accept risk and challenge, because through risk and challenge we grow both in worldly wisdom and spiritual strength.

In the Bahamas, Templeton promoted spirituality in a number of ways. His Templeton Foundation gave scholarships to ministers in the Bahamas for study both there and at New Jersey's Princeton Theological Seminary. Recently, in memory of his mother, Templeton founded Templeton Theological Seminary, the first school for the education of Christian ministers in the Bahamas. Also, each year the foundation sponsors lectures in the Bahamas by the winners of the Templeton Prize for Progress in Religion.

The Templeton Prize is John Templeton's most ambitious contribution to understanding the religious life. Through it, his ultimate purpose—to help millions of people in all nations to benefit from learning about the major new spiritual developments throughout the world—seems well on the road to accomplishment. Not surprisingly, given the force of his belief, his entire family has joined in the effort. Templeton's wife, all five of their children, and his brother Harvey are trustees of the Templeton Foundation.

Templeton, John W. Galbraith, and Thomas L. Hansberger operate an investment counsel corporation that manages over $10 billion of securities worldwide in private accounts and public investment mutual funds owned by over 500,000 investors in many nations. Templeton, Galbraith & Hansberger Ltd. and its associates have offices in

Nassau; St. Petersburg and Fort Lauderdale, Florida; Toronto; London; and Hong Kong. Its shares trade actively on the London Stock Exchange.

The frontier lies in the future, and success-bound people welcome the future just as they welcome change generally. We Americans were led to believe that with the opening up of the West, there were no new frontiers to discover. Nothing could be further from the truth. Every day new fields develop or grow more sophisticated, which means increased opportunities. But you must be willing to work hard and to risk. You must be prepared and eager to confront challenge, private and professional.

If you look to the future as a vast, exciting, and still unexplored territory, you are on your way to becoming a successful person.

After reading and reviewing Step 20, you should ask yourself the following questions:

1. Am I open to change?
2. Am I eager to travel to new places?
3. Am I eager to meet new people?
4. Am I receptive to new ways to do things that will improve my performance?
5. Do others consider me a flexible person with an open mind?
6. Do I make an attempt to bring my professional and spiritual lives into harmony?
7. Do I feel that I'm prepared to deal with adversity?

Remember: Reaching out takes many forms, all of them important. You reach out by giving to others. You reach out by understanding and appreciating others. And you reach out in your search for new frontiers. They are all important ways to grow into a more successful and happy human being, and they are connected, one to the other.

STEP 21

SEEKING SOLUTIONS

SUCCESS GOES to those people who seek solutions rather than problems, and nowhere is this more evident than in a business career. An employer is more likely to promote those who never come forward with a problem for which they do not offer—or actively seek—a solution.

In all areas of life, people who are problem-laden cast a deadening influence on themselves and others. They stress the negative rather than the positive. They need to learn that inventive thinking results from a constant search for solutions.

A choice of career is the first major solution the success-bound person must seek. The wisest course is to choose an area where you can become an expert. Ninety-nine percent of us can become an expert at something.

If you have any doubt about where your abilities lie, take various aptitude tests. Talk to your teachers and friends about yourself, asking them to assess your strengths and weaknesses. Go through a telephone directory and mark those businesses and professions where you sense your talents lie.

But never take a passive and negative approach to your own self-assessment. Don't assume that you have no special talent, because you do. We all do.

Once you have chosen a career path, study and work harder than others so that you can become the very best at what you do. Only one person will reach the very highest rung, but by trying hard most of us can achieve the upper 10 percent and thereby lead happy and productive lives.

It is sad to see people envy the talents of others. They are creating problems for themselves, not solutions. Whatever path you take, tell yourself it is the very best path there is, and envy no one. Try to learn as much as can be learned in your field. Experiment and originate; try to extend the frontiers of knowledge in that field.

Working at the top level in any field, however humble, gives a person self-confidence. In turn, the self-confidence will attract the confidence of others. It is in such a way that success feeds on itself and creates more success.

Sometimes it happens that, having become an expert in one area, technological or other changes occur that render your job redundant. Accordingly; it is wise to move as soon as possible to where the opportunities still exist. Do not remain in a position that is no longer useful. If, in fact, you lose your job, it is vital to have an open-minded and flexible attitude about possible career solutions. Finding the suitable new job is a job in itself. The solution is to work eight hours a day, sending out résumés, answering classified advertisements, and setting up appointments.

In the last analysis, however, no true solutions are possible without recourse to God. When John Templeton's children were teenagers, he wrote an essay for them in which he said, in part:

> Some people put their trust in their wealth. Others in their beauty. Others in their intellect. Still others in their strength. But you're likely to be disappointed if you put your total trust in any of these.
>
> The giver of each of these is God, not you. You have been given strength or beauty or intelligence in order to let you experience humility and duty. Certainly not pride. There are people who say, "I earn my money by hard work," which is true in a limited sense. But who gave them the ability to work hard?
>
> We should realize that God is in charge. Ultimately we must call on God for solutions. His purposes are wiser than ours. Excessive worry only increases the problems, whereas prayer and thanksgiving to God for help in solving problems often lead to surprising solutions.
>
> My mother reared my brother and me on the philosophy that only God could protect us from mistake and harm. She could not. For example, one time we were taking a canoe trip down a small and dangerous river. We couldn't call home

at sundown as planned because our canoe had sunk. Four hours after nightfall we finally hiked to a phone. Our mother promptly drove out and picked us up. She hadn't worried about us. She knew that we were children of God and that he would watch over us. There was no reason for her to worry endlessly.

Since then I have always tried to think up every possible solution to a problem and then go to sleep at night, confident that through prayer God will guide me.

Every age produces individuals who possess an extraordinary capacity for acquiring wealth. They seem to possess a talent for accumulating material goods at a rapid rate. Less successful people—including those who may have great aspirations to "make it big" but have not yet reached real wealth—often wonder: "Do I really have what it takes to reach the top? Will I be capable of finding strategies and arriving at solutions that will secure my family's financial well-being?"

John Templeton and his parents were severely pinched by the depression of 1932. Yet this relatively poor southern boy had the seeds of success in his personality, and he nurtured those seeds into full bloom in his adult life as an investment sage. How did he arrive at the solutions that made this possible?

From the beginning, part of Templeton's formula for

material success was simplicity itself. He had studied both history and economics with great care. He worked hard, and he was not afraid to discover new frontiers. Thus he positioned himself to arrive at solutions, whose effects are still being felt by his clients more than forty years later.

To quote from a talk he gave to shareholders at the July 1985 annual meeting in Toronto:

> I remember a time when every bank in America closed and 3,000 banks never reopened. In those days there was no government guarantee of bank deposits. There was no social security. There was no unemployment insurance. There was no feeling on the part of voters that the government should help.
>
> Banks are not likely to fail again because governments will rescue them. But every method of rescue we have studied so far, worldwide over twenty years, results in more money in the hands of the public. It results in more inflation.
>
> In 1931, when there were bankruptcies of 3,000 banks, the thing to do to protect one's assets was to invest in money—in cash—because in those days you had deflation. Now you don't have deflation, you have inflation. So if you want to protect your wealth against this tremendous problem, invest in things that are not fixed in terms of so many dollars like a bank deposit, or a bond, or a

> mortgage. Invest in those things that represent a share in the ownership of a productive asset and may go up in value as the dollar loses its purchasing power.
>
> Those things are mainly real estate and common stocks.

And therein lay John Templeton's offered solution to the financial problems of investors worldwide. He said, in effect: "Don't stand by while your money dwindles in value in savings accounts. Make your money work for you. Become a capitalist by buying into other companies through the purchase of common stock in a mutual funds plan."

John Templeton's upbringing implanted in him the inner drive and personal values necessary to reach the highest level of performance as an investor. He learned how to be comfortable with his wealth. He is a self-made man who lacked the benefit of a family tradition of "old money" and philanthropy, but he has avoided the danger of being corrupted by money, because he has learned the secret of "living successfully with success." Indeed, he provides an outstanding example of how a person's wealth can become a satisfying extension of his inner drives and values. He found solutions for reconciling his business success with his powerful religious convictions.

King Midas, in the famous myth, once encountered the forest god Silenus, who was a close companion and mentor of Dionysus, the Greek god of wine, fertility, and revelry.

Silenus wandered drunkenly into Midas's royal gardens, got lost, and finally was rescued by the king. Dionysus was so happy when Midas returned with his friend that he promised to grant Midas his deepest wish. Midas, a materialistic man, asked for the power to turn everything he touched into gold.

This wish was bestowed on him. But the problem was that everything he touched, without exception, turned to gold, including his food and drink.

Midas was lucky. He returned to Dionysus who agreed to remove the spell. His almost-fatal mistake was that he became consumed by a desire to build up a store of immense wealth without considering the consequences.

Wealth, for the successful person, however, has a purpose that goes beyond mere accumulation. Otherwise, material goods can actually careen out of control, turn on their possessors, and ultimately destroy them.

Unlike Midas, whose wealth exerted a negative force, Templeton had a positive solution to the "problem" of money; he would use his material gains in a way that would benefit others. His attitude toward his worldly success involved a sense of stewardship, a belief that what you have is not actually yours but is held in trust for the good of all humanity.

John Templeton has never been satisfied to be merely wealthy. He has also worked hard, studied hard, and always prayed to be loving and giving. For him, these are the qualities that make for success. Through the years, he has kept to a great vision and a high standard—to seek the original, the spiritual, and the love and understanding of God.

Therein lies his success.

Therein can lie yours.

To summarize Step 21:

1. Be a problem solver, not a problem maker.
2. Choose a career where you have a chance to become an expert.
3. Never remain in a position that is no longer useful, but quickly begin the search for possible career solutions.
4. If you are faced with a difficult problem to solve, pray to God for guidance.
5. Beware of the Midas example: Money is never an end in itself but only the means to an end.
6. Use your material gains in ways that will benefit others.

The basic lesson to be learned from Step 21 is that you can live successfully with success. By following the six points just listed, your wealth, no matter how much or little, can become a satisfying extension of your inner drives and values.

SUMMING UP THE TEMPLETON PLAN

By reviewing the twenty-one steps that make up The Templeton Plan, it is hoped that readers will form a mental map of the guideposts to follow as they advance along the success course.

In the introduction, we discussed motivation. We learned that the successful individual will tackle every endeavor from a solid ethical and religious base. It is John Templeton's firm belief, based on his years of working with some of the world's most successful people, that strong spiritual values will help us as we search for financial success and a happy and fulfilled life.

Leaders who follow spiritual principles inspire enthusiasm in others. They tend to run better-functioning businesses. Their employees are loyal to them. They are the type of leaders—like John Templeton himself—who often begin and end business meetings with prayer. They are the type of leaders who treat each employee just as they themselves would hope to be treated.

John Templeton believes that if your basic values are rooted in religion, financial success is more likely to follow.

It is important, as developed in Step 1, to learn and practice the laws of life. Among the laws of life are truthfulness, perseverance, joy, enthusiasm, humility, and altruism.

A person who hopes to be successful in any endeavor must adhere to these laws. By incorporating them into your code of behavior, you're on your way to becoming a fulfilled human being. You'll learn to give freely of yourself and to love without fear. Following the laws of life will give you a greater chance of succeeding at anything you attempt to do.

In order to use what you have, it is important to learn something new each day. Step 2 demonstrated that learning is a lifetime endeavor. We should monitor our daily behavior and make certain that we don't end up like John Templeton's friend who, upon graduating from high school, never read another book.

We must continue to read, to learn, to experience new feelings and ideas. To show initiative at an early age. To observe others. To listen carefully to others. To use whatever degree of intelligence we possess to the fullest. We may not all be born with equal abilities, but by using what we have wisely and well, we can achieve success and happiness.

We learned in Step 3 that the best way to help yourself is to help others. You must ask yourself whether or not you are using your talents in the wisest way, which means for others as well as yourself. You must ask yourself whether or not your work is helping at least one other human being.

John Templeton learned from Jesus' parable of the talents, as set forth in Matthew, that God gave talents to each of us and that he expects us to use what talents we are given to the utmost. Through our talents we can create beauty. We can help others. We can manufacture a product that lasts. The greatest good of all is to help others discover and develop their own abilities.

Step 4 asked us to examine our virtues, to draw up lists of them, and assign them values. Successful people live their virtues consciously. A partial list of virtues would include gentleness, honesty, bravery, loyalty, and hope. If you place a certain virtue—say, honesty—at the top of your list, that tells you a great deal about yourself. It is important to practice all the virtues, but it is also important to know what they mean in our lives.

Success-bound people understand that you don't become happy by concentrating on trying to be happy. They have learned the valuable lesson, which we explored in Step 5, that happiness is achieved by what you do. If you please others, you will please yourself. Happiness and success are in the giving, not the getting. They are in the production, not the consumption. So set new goals for yourself constantly. Always remain active. And if you don't look for happiness, but give it, it will seek you out.

Step 6 provided us with many examples of how to find the positive in every negative, of how to live in harmony with others in ways that lead to productive change. It is important to shun gossip, to avoid comparisons, to read literature that inspires you, and to welcome each day as a new start, an adventure, a seminar in living. Finding the positive is partly a matter of perspective; you should always view your glass as half full, not half empty.

Investing yourself in your work, as we learned in Step 7, is the true elixir of life. An idea is only an idea until you subject it to the test of hard work. People who invest themselves in their work are the ones who turn problems into opportunities. They carry reading material with them wherever they go and even a tape recorder so that they can note their thoughts in free moments between appointments. They know how to defer pleasure until the job at hand is done.

Step 8 made the point that there is no such thing as luck over the span of an entire career. The main ingredients of "luck" are careful planning, plenty of perseverance, and the use of imagination. In the final analysis, what we call luck is what you manage to make of all the options available to you.

You must always be prepared, make certain that you've done your homework, and that your goals are worthy ones, and you will have the kind of constant and lifelong "luck" that has nothing to do with cards or roulette wheels.

Step 9 examined two key principles of success and happiness: honesty and perseverance. Success-bound people finish what they begin. They handle all their business relationships as a sacred trust. They give what they promise and never cut corners. By investing in the virtues of honesty and perseverance, you will find that others are more likely to invest in you.

As we discovered in Step 10, making time your servant is a way of putting the other person first. Promptness is politeness and consideration. It is also good business.

Success-bound people learn early in their careers to avoid the *mañana* habit. They do today whatever can possibly be done today and try not to put off anything until tomorrow. Tomorrow, after all, can mean next week, or next month, or perhaps never. Successful people always squeeze all that they can into today's schedule, knowing that tomorrow will be equally full of new deadlines and challenges.

John Templeton has developed a principle that he calls "the doctrine of the extra ounce," which was discussed in Step 11. When he was still young, he came to realize that people who are moderately successful do nearly as much work as those who are outstandingly successful. The difference in effort is small but significant—a matter of giving the extra ounce. Those who are bound to succeed give seventeen ounces to the pint instead of sixteen. And the success they achieve thereby is out of all proportion to that one ounce.

So you must make that extra effort. You must give just a little more than the next person. The result is better quality, a higher level of performance, and a reputation for getting the job done right.

Thrift, examined in Step 12, is a vital component of success and happiness. People who conserve their resources to best advantage are less likely to have to borrow; we must take a hard look at the perils involved in borrowing too heavily. Those who are deeply in debt in times of economic crisis are the first to lose their holdings. Thrifty people make a budget and stick to it. They save something from every paycheck. They search for bargains in small as well as big items. They are not impulse buyers but consider each purchase carefully.

In Step 13 we studied methods for moving onwards and upwards. The key to progress is change—intelligent, informed change. Successful people are never afraid to try something new. As Thomas Edison said, "If you are doing something the same way you did it twenty years ago, then there must be a better way." You have to be willing to pit yourself against your past performance, to welcome the entrepreneurial spirit within yourself, and strive constantly to become the best-informed and most creative person in your field.

Controlling your thoughts for effective action was the subject of Step 14. Successful and happy people learn to control their thoughts. By controlling them, to quote John Templeton, "you can make your mind a garden of indescribably beautiful flowers instead of a weed patch."

Templeton advocates what he calls the "crowding-out" method of thought control. You fill your mind with positive and productive thoughts in order to crowd out the negative ones. By employing this method, your mind will be clear, your thinking will be directed toward your goal, and you will approach every problem with a "can-do" attitude. Remember: You are what you think.

Step 15 took up the subject of loving as the essential ingredient in our lives. We learned that it is important to learn to love and understand our enemies. Loving those who love us is easy. Loving our enemies is difficult, but Jesus has stressed its importance. We must also allow ourselves to love ourselves. Self-love radiates out to others and then reflects back to us through the love others show us. The way to be in touch with our common humanity is through the kindness and patience we bring to all of our relationships, both business and personal.

In Step 16 we studied ways to maximize the power of our faith. The parable of the workers in the vineyard gave us a dramatic lesson in not begrudging others their good fortune. On the contrary, we must learn to exult in the good fortune of others, just as we must be quick to express empathy. We learned that when your faith is strong, your prospects for happiness and success are excellent.

Step 17 stressed the importance of prayer in the lives of successful and happy people. Prayer helps you to avoid pettiness and needless controversy. Prayer helps you to act in a more responsible manner and opens your mind to clear thinking. Prayer helps you to become truly humble, to realize that you're only a tiny fraction of God's universe, and to live in harmony with God's purposes.

By making a deep and sincere effort to be one with God through prayer, everything you do in life will turn out better, and success is more likely to seek you out.

In Step 18 we studied the importance of giving as a way of life. Giving, for Templeton, is a natural concomitant of prayer. We should give to charity. Give help. Give encouragement. Give carefully reasoned advice. The abilities, intelligence, and material success we have been blessed with should be returned to the world in some form that will benefit humanity.

Step 19 examined the importance of humility in the successful and happy life. It emphasized that we must teach ourselves to experience awe in the face of the many mysteries that surround us. As John Templeton has said, "The God who created and sustained his evolving universe through eons of progress and development has not placed our generation at the tag end of the creative process. He has placed us at a new beginning. We are here for the future."

To be successful we must try to build our souls in imitation of the Creator. We must appreciate other people. We must express our faith in God in all situations. Our spirits must be humble. Through deep humility and love of God and humanity, we can develop a victorious personality.

The person who is willing to say yes to experience is the person who discovers new frontiers. Step 20 teaches us to welcome, not fear, the frontier. Success-bound people have to believe in themselves, because the frontier exists inside of them. They possess deep religious faith that helps them to accept challenges and new experiences. Through good times and bad they will embrace the future with open arms. People bound for success and happiness will view the future as an exciting and still unexplored territory and move toward the frontier with enthusiasm.

We must be problem solvers, not problem makers, as we

learned in Step 21. The negative thinker stresses problems, while the inventive thinker seeks solutions. Problem solving is a necessary art as long as life lasts, and it's important to become a creative practitioner of that art. Choose a career where you have a chance to excel. Faced with a difficult problem to solve, pray to God for guidance. Always remember that by constantly seeking solutions—creative ones—you are learning how to live successfully with success.

Living successfully with success is perhaps the ultimate solution for the person who reaches that pinnacle. John Templeton has never been satisfied with mere wealth. He has prayed to be loving and giving. Through the years, he has sought the love and understanding of God and God's children. The solution to great wealth is to give. The solution to ignorance is to learn. And the solution to misunderstanding and negativism is to practice the art of loving.

John Templeton would sum up in these words the life plan that he believes has enabled him to achieve success and happiness:

> Twenty-one steps is an arbitrary number. There are most likely hundreds of steps to success and happiness, just as there are hundreds of laws of life. But these are the steps that have worked for me. These are ones I've tested and I know are sound. I can pass them on to readers with the happy knowledge that if they helped me in my life, they can surely help them in theirs.

Trying to follow these twenty-one steps every moment of every day for much of my life has been worth it. They have made me a better person than I might otherwise have been. We are all God's creatures; we are fallible; we make mistakes. To grow within ourselves, to reach our full potential as human beings, we are all in need of help along the way. I'm glad I learned the principles outlined in this book, because they helped me both in my professional and personal lives.

My hope is that you, too, and your children and grandchildren, by learning these twenty-one principles, plus many more, may achieve more happiness, usefulness, and success.